CW00469135

MIND YOUR MANNERS

MIND YOUR MANNERS

An Insider's Guide to Social Fluency

SARA JANE HO

bluebird
books for life

First published in the USA 2024 by Hachette Go, an imprint of Hachette Books

First published in the UK 2024 by Bluebird
an imprint of Pan Macmillan
The Smithson, 6 Briset Street, London EC1M 5NR
EU representative: Macmillan Publishers Ireland Ltd, 1st Floor,
The Liffey Trust Centre, 117–126 Sheriff Street Upper,
Dublin 1, D01 YC43
Associated companies throughout the world
www.panmacmillan.com

ISBN 978-1-0350-3719-3

Copyright © Sara Jane Ho 2024

The right of Sara Jane Ho to be identified as the
Author of this work has been asserted by her in accordance
with the Copyright, Designs and Patents Act 1988.

All rights reserved. No part of this publication may be reproduced,
stored in a retrieval system, or transmitted, in any form, or by any means
(electronic, mechanical, photocopying, recording or otherwise)
without the prior written permission of the publisher.

Pan Macmillan does not have any control over, or any responsibility for,
any author or third-party websites referred to in or on this book.

1 3 5 7 9 8 6 4 2

A CIP catalogue record for this book is available from the British Library.

Print book interior design by Sheryl Kober.

Printed and bound by CPI Group (UK) Ltd, Croydon, CR0 4YY

This book is sold subject to the condition that it shall not, by way of
trade or otherwise, be lent, hired out, or otherwise circulated without
the publisher's prior consent in any form of binding or cover other than
that in which it is published and without a similar condition including
this condition being imposed on the subsequent purchaser.

The information provided in this book is not an alternative to medical advice
from your doctor or other professional healthcare provider. You should not
delay in seeking medical advice, disregard medical advice or discontinue
any medical treatment because of the information provided in this book.

Visit **www.panmacmillan.com/bluebird** to read more about all our books
and to buy them. You will also find features, author interviews and
news of any author events, and you can sign up for e-newsletters
so that you're always first to hear about our new releases.

In memory of my mother, always alive in my heart,
for my father, a true gentleman,
and for Flora, who taught me the beauty of kindness.

CONTENTS

INTRODUCTION

"The Etiquette Guru Who Broke Up with a Boyfriend over Text." When I saw the headline of the *New York Times* Style section profile, I cringed for a moment. But only for a moment. Then I laughed. Paired with a photo of me spearing a cupcake with my knife, it playfully summed up my brand of etiquette: sticking a fork (or knife!) into the idea that etiquette is all about which fork to use.

So what *do* I believe etiquette is about? In a word: connection.

Etiquette, as I often say, is the glue that holds society together. And we could certainly use more of that because we're coming unstuck. Look around. Or better yet, take a look inside. I hear reports from my etiquette students, my social media followers, and many fans of my Netflix series *Mind Your Manners* that they're anxious. They're lonely and unsure about how to reach out to others. Maybe you feel the same, because statistics bear out that we're in the midst of a mental health catastrophe. The pandemic only worsened a preexisting shadow epidemic of loneliness, and millennials and Gen Z are suffering the most from this anxiety and isolation.

If you're reading this, maybe your social skills took a hit during the pandemic and never recovered. Perhaps you tell yourself that you're fine as you are. It might feel good to curl up on the couch in your pajamas with your phone, but we humans are remarkably bad at determining what actually makes us happy. We are social creatures and need connection, and much of our withdrawal is motivated by fear.

Therapy alone won't solve our mental health problems because many of those problems are social rather than individual. I received an email from a first-year student at my alma mater, Georgetown University, who described my outlook on etiquette as "the utmost form of wellness, a way to promote genuine and healthy individual growth." I was flattered, of course, but it also struck a chord. Etiquette works like behavior therapy: it improves our mood from the outside in. Change starts when we change out of our pajamas, step away from our screens, and interact face-to-face. It might not seem worth taking the risk to get back out there, but I assure you, it is.

At the beginning of my Netflix show, I made a promise to viewers: "Come with me, and you'll know what to do anywhere, with anyone, in any situation." I wrote Mind Your Manners to fulfill and expand upon that promise. I want to grant you a wish: the knowledge of how to behave perfectly in every situation. I want to help free you from social anxiety so you can have fun in every aspect of your life—not only with your friends and family, but also at work and in your romantic relationships.

I want, in other words, the opportunity to teach you social fluency. And as I know from learning multiple languages, the first step to achieving fluency is good instruction. That's where all my studying, training, and hard work come in.

So, what does social fluency mean, exactly? Two things: (1) being able to read people and situations with accuracy and speed, and (2) being able to interact with others in a smooth, effective,

2

and confident way. What I learned through navigating many cultures since early childhood is that we all move among many *microcultures* every day, even when we never leave home. Social Life and Friendship, Work, Dating and Relationships, Family, and Food and Travel are all different microcultures, so they constitute the five divisions of the book. Every microculture has its own set of precepts and its own dialect, and I'll break down the steps necessary to achieve fluency in each one.

Unlike traditional etiquette, which was born in the seventeenth-century court of Versailles and refers to the "etiquettes" or labels that the king posted throughout the palace to enforce strict decorum, contemporary etiquette is *contextual*. To be your best self in each situation means learning to read its context quickly and accurately. Interacting smoothly and confidently at dinner with your boss will look different from being at ease meeting your boyfriend's crew for the first time. Inevitably, sticky situations will arise. My mission in *Mind Your Manners* is to help you jump everyday relationship hurdles and politely handle the not-so-polite situations that can cause social shutdown, whether in real life or in the digital realm.

Obviously, I wasn't born knowing how to behave in every situation. Etiquette began as a survival tactic for me. Because I spent the first thirty-plus years of my life straddling different countries and cultures, I needed to become adept at cracking the code of whatever social situation I landed in. Even as a child, abruptly barred from going barefoot when we moved from Papua New Guinea to England, I started to understand that etiquette is contextual. Of course, I wouldn't have been able to put that into words, but I recognized early that I had to develop skills for decoding a broad range of cultures and microcultures—and do it fast. Eventually, I came to think of myself as a microcultural anthropologist. Even now, wherever I go, I see myself as in the field. I'm always observing and asking myself, "What are the codes of conduct here? How are people behaving?"

What began as a survival tactic became my life's work when I graduated from Harvard Business School in 2012 and founded China's first finishing school in Beijing in 2013. Since then, the most common question I've been asked is why I teach etiquette. Sometimes people are curious about the subject itself, but more often they're curious about why a gregarious Harvard MBA with a wicked sense of humor chose to teach it. The official answer is that I teach international etiquette because it satisfies a need: as a result of China's economic reform policies in 1978, many people found themselves with enormous prosperity decades later but without the social skills to navigate their new way of life. But the deeper answer is that it gives me the opportunity to pass on my mother's legacy.

My mother was an entertainment industry executive in Hong Kong. Elegant, energetic, and very demanding, she was also an incomparably charming hostess. My earliest memories are of her welcoming friends and family into our home. She threw a great Christmas party and took pleasure in the smallest details of entertaining—from the guest list and menu to the table settings and decoration. These gatherings were magical because she was a shameless flirt and inveterate prankster who injected fun into every gathering. She was also unequaled at smoothing over awkwardness and putting others at ease. As I mentioned, she was demanding, a quintessential Tiger Mom (before there was such a term), always ready with a kick under the table to alert me to a duty I had overlooked or was not performing properly.

When I was twenty-one, I lost my mother to cancer. My father stopped entertaining after she died, and our previously lively home felt empty. One day I realized I could use what my mother had taught me about the etiquette of entertaining to gather friends and family together again. I couldn't bring her back, but I could bring warmth and energy back into our home. Practicing etiquette and teaching it to others is my way of keeping her memory alive, not only the part of her that welcomed others so generously, but also the part that kicked me under the table when I wasn't attending properly to their needs!

Rather than limiting myself to Western-style etiquette, I draw examples from various international cultures and customs in the following pages. The etiquette you'll find there is a set of dynamic and situation-specific tools rather than strict and unforgiving rules. They will help you navigate awkward social situations, and even more importantly they will free you from the illusion that your cocoon is a cozy permanent residence. Cocoons are meant to be places of temporary refuge, where transformation takes place. Even if we don't aspire to be social butterflies, we all crave the freedom to express our best selves in every aspect of our lives. *Mind Your Manners* will give you the skills to attract connections rather than wait for the world to come to you. (And these include some Miss Machiavelli techniques to help you get ahead—because being well-mannered shouldn't mean being outmaneuvered.)

Above all, etiquette is about putting people at ease, and that includes yourself.

PART ONE

SOCIAL LIFE AND FRIENDSHIP

True friends stab you in the front.

—OSCAR WILDE

Your Best Social Self

As I explained in the introduction, we move among several micro-cultures every day, even if we never travel. A microculture—whether it be social, work, dating, or family—is a context. Thinking like an anthropologist will help you crack the code of each one and present your best self. With practice, you will lose your "accent" and translate fluently among the many microcultures that make up your life.

Social life is a microculture, and friendship is its most important subset. The dictionary defines social life as "the part of a person's time spent doing enjoyable things with others." Urban Dictionary, which is often a more accurate reflection of collective attitudes, calls it "something you probably don't have" or "torture dressed as fun." So which is it?

One point in favor of Urban Dictionary is that we use "social" as shorthand for our social media accounts (as in "my social") more often than we do to describe our lives. A recent study found that since the pandemic became endemic, 35 percent of people are less interested in socializing than they were before. This has harmed our mental health, but social fluency is a way of fighting back.

How much social contact we desire, and what kind, has to do with our personality. For extroverts, the usual advice to "get out there" makes sense. But for introverts or people with social anxiety, those words induce panic. No matter which camp you fall into, this chapter will teach you how to enjoy the social swim and help you negotiate the sometimes tricky challenges of friendship, both digitally and in real life.

SOCIAL LIFE

The First Secret of Social Fluency: Reading the Air

To achieve social fluency and feel confident in any social situation, you need to be able to "read" people and situations with accuracy. One way is mastering the subtle art of "reading the air." This Japanese expression means picking up on nonverbal cues like body language and tone of voice to get a "read" on what is being deliberately left unsaid. Like other Asian countries, Japan is what is known as a high-context culture, where meaning is mutually created through active listening and reading between the lines. The United States, by contrast, is a low-context culture, which values clear and direct communication.

Reading the air is similar to what Americans call picking up "vibes," or what the Chinese call *qi chang* (*qi* means energy; *chang* means field). The *qi* (pronounced "chee") of a room is invisible but palpable. You know this if you've ever walked into a gathering where something is "not quite right." When you feel that disharmony, you are tapping into your body's *qi*, or native intelligence. I am admittedly oversensitive when it comes to detecting qi, but maybe that comes with the territory of being an etiquette teacher! Some people walk into a party and head straight for the bar. I walk in and notice whose glass is empty. Part of it might be my obsession with worrying about everyone's comfort (I can still feel my mother kicking me under the table when someone's teacup was empty). But it goes deeper than that. For me, seeing someone standing without a drink or a conversation partner is like hearing a baby crying. It arouses an immediate and urgent need to do something about it.

In any social situation, ask yourself, what's wrong with this picture? How can I fix it? Who should be introduced to whom, who looks uncomfortable, who would benefit from what connection, what problems are brewing, what opportunities are presenting themselves, who needs to be encouraged, and who should be reined in? People have varying degrees of sensitivity to these "vibes," but everyone has the ability to sharpen their observational skills and develop a more subtle awareness of how others may feel. And thinking about others has the added benefit of taking the focus off any social anxiety you might be experiencing.

Every conversation is like a story. It needs a warm-up, a climax, and a cooldown. Don't end a conversation too abruptly. Guide it to a close by signaling that you're about to wrap up. "Well, I'm going to head out now, I have another meeting. It was great to see you!"

You Never Get a Second Chance to Make a First Impression

Let me rephrase that. You never get a *second* to make a first impression. That wasn't a typo. People form a first impression in a tenth of a second. And first impressions are remarkably stable over time. Our brains are designed to conserve energy, so we are vulnerable to something called confirmation bias. Once we form an opinion, we look for evidence to support it. It takes a lot of information to get us to change our minds. There are a lot of references on the internet to a fabled "Harvard study" claiming that it takes eight positive encounters to undo one negative first impression. Too bad it doesn't exist. There's actually no set number, but the Harvard myth offers a good metaphor—it's much easier to make a good impression than to try to undo a bad one.

I'm frequently asked how you make a good first impression on a partner's friends or family, and the story of Ian never fails to pop into my mind. He was one of my best friends in college, and one long weekend, he invited me and a few friends to stay at his house in Malibu. On the first day, his mother cooked us chicken for dinner. At the end of the meal, his parents asked us if we wanted seconds. "I would love some," I said, and helped myself to the smallest piece.

In Chinese we have a phrase called *ba wo hao du*, which means you must learn how to stay within the boundary. Know how to move forward without being aggressive. Although Ian's mother made a mean chicken, I didn't really need to have seconds. But she was a homemaker, and I could tell that cooking for her family was important to her. Being raised in a Chinese family where parents showed love for their children by cooking and children showed their appreciation by eating, I performed this

11

ritual toward Ian's mother at the age of eighteen without even thinking. Ian was one of my best friends, so I wanted to make a good impression on his family.

"Oh my god, my dad LOVED you," Ian said afterward. "After you left, he kept talking about how you had seconds, but took the smallest piece." His dad was a Los Angeles County Superior Court judge for sixteen years, very studied and very serious. For years to come, Ian would call me every time his dad mentioned the story as affirmation that he approved of me as Ian's friend.

I had a second helping to show my compliments, but I took the smallest piece to show I wasn't greedy. In one meal, I had stayed within the limits—pleasing but maintaining deference.

How to Be a Social Magnet

Socializing requires an initial effort to get over the hump of inertia, and getting out of our pajamas can be a real challenge. Sometimes it feels simpler to stay on the couch and scroll through our phones than to engage in meaningful conversation with others. But, just like a muscle, our socializing skills atrophy if we don't use them.

Ruby, a friend who lives near a beautiful state park, reached out to me for a coffee date and a hike. We had a group chat with another friend, Vivian, whom I was hoping to see at the same time. When Ruby arrived alone, I asked her where Vivian was. "I didn't bother asking her," she replied. "She never initiates anything, and even when we ask her out she doesn't always come. I think she just prefers to stay at home." I think of this as a cautionary tale about what happens if we get too comfortable in our little nests.

We humans are often wrong about what truly provides us with happiness. We think we feel safe if we stay at home alone night after night, but what we are actually feeling is numb. The anxiety is still there, humming along underneath. Spending time with others is essential for physical and mental health, but we will likely avoid it if it seems like a chore. That's why we're so grateful for the charming ones, the people who draw us out of our shells.

I have a proposition for you. What about trying to *be* that person? Instead of waiting to be sought out, be sought after. Luckily, the path to cultivating personal magnetism, also known as charm, is simpler than you might imagine.

People think of charm as a magical quality, something you must be born with, but that is far from the truth. Charm is a form of "soft power." Unlike charisma, which is a divine gift only bestowed upon a select few, personal magnetism is available to all of us. The only requirement for charm is to be truly interested in others. As the insightful mystery writer P. D. James wrote, "No one has [charm] who isn't capable of genuinely liking others, at least at the actual moment of meeting and speaking. Charm is always genuine; it may be superficial but it isn't false."

The secret of charm is making every person feel that they have a special connection with you. Politicians are masters of this art. They can hold people spellbound with their seemingly undivided attention, even if only for an instant. If they can do it, then so can you—with a few helpful tips!

Eye contact is key (but not staring, which is never a good "look"), and careful listening is essential. What people call the art of conversation is nine parts listening, one part talking. And charm always includes a dash of the unexpected, which is why it's so hard to put into words. As a Supreme Court justice famously said about pornography, you might not know how to define it, but you know it when you see it.

On the other hand, there is such a thing as too much charm, which is sleaze. I discovered this when I went on my first and last date with a notorious Lebanese banker in Hong Kong. I'd heard enough women say, "If you haven't been hit on by him, you haven't eaten white rice," to know I should be wary. But he was incredibly smooth and knew how to pay compliments. It didn't take long for me to notice, however, that he was looking at everyone except me when he talked to me, his eyes scanning left and right as if he were watching a tennis match. It made me feel insecure that I couldn't hold his attention even for the length of a brief conversation. I didn't go out with him again, and I wasn't surprised to hear from other friends—male and female—that he had made them feel the same way. "Charm" only works if it's genuine.

> "The opposite of talking isn't listening—the opposite of talking is waiting."
>
> —FRAN LEBOWITZ

So start small. Especially if you are shy or have social anxiety, reaching out might be a challenge. One of my students, Jing, was painfully shy and spoke so softly that during class I brought her out of her comfort zone by asking her to shout (which really was just everyone else's normal). I gave her a thirty-day homework assignment of initiating conversation with a stranger once a day—whether it be the security guard in her building, someone sitting next to her on the plane, or a server at a restaurant—and told her to report to me weekly. Although in the beginning she had to force herself to speak with strangers, by the end of the first week, she was so excited about her assignment that she climbed into the front seat of a taxi so she could chat with the driver! For the first time in her life, she said, someone she spoke to described her as a happy and cheerful girl.

Be brave and invite an acquaintance to accompany you to a concert, an art exhibit, or something out of left field like Comic-Con, even if they have no clue about where they're going. Shake up their lives a little. There must be something you're passionate about, whether it's manga or opera or a hike in the woods. Be interesting as well as interested, and secure a return invitation. Venture out of your cocoon, and before long you'll find you're a social butterfly—in demand and comfortable everywhere.

> Inaction is more harmful than rejection. If something is worth having, it's worth the risk.

Practice Nonsexual Flirting

If you Google "flirting," the top result, from Wikipedia, is "a social and sexual behavior involving body language, or spoken or written communication. It is used to suggest interest in a deeper relationship with another person and, if done playfully, for amusement." Take out the word "sexual" and you have a formula for creating chemistry and warmth with another person. I flirt with everybody and anybody, whether they are eighty years old or eight. I grew up watching my mother, who was a great nonsexual flirt. She flirted with her boss, with her staff, with clients, and with vendors. She knew how to ramp up the energy and let everyone have fun. She was a great prankster, too. My dad also did this but in a more kindly, inquisitive way than my mother, with her charm and impishness. His social flirting was more mild-mannered, tempered with English reserve.

Another of my role models in this regard was Jenny, my sophomore year roommate. She was a blond and blue-eyed southern belle from Atlanta, who always had a smile and a "Hi, how ya doin'?" for everybody who crossed her path. She was kind and sweet, and her greetings were from the heart. One day a boy in our dorm named Steven stopped me in the hallway. "Hey, Sara," he said, "what's the name of your roommate again? I think she likes me." I was shocked because she was totally out of his league, so I wasn't sure where he got this idea, but of course I didn't show it. I told him her name and asked, "Really, what makes you think so?" "Because," he said, "she smiled at me the other day when I was leaving the elevator." He mistook Jenny's friendliness for flirtation, but there was no harm done. It made him feel good about himself, and it acquired Jenny another admirer.

It is important to be clear not to confuse one type of interest for another, but showing warmth and playfulness toward another person heightens the energy in an interaction, and results in more pleasure for yourself as well.

Push People Beyond Their Comfort Zone

Daily life can be boring, and people find it energizing and refreshing to be challenged in little ways. I've often been told, "I can't believe you got away with asking that!" but people rarely take offense. The main secret of pushing the envelope is to do it out of genuine interest, and with a smile. You can't go blundering in and ask anything that's on your mind. That would just be rude. There's a fine line between being curious and being intrusive.

Let me give you an example from a recent lunch I had with some older cousins I hadn't seen in several years. They are in their forties and fifties, and most of them are married, but my cousin Ronald is not. After they finished talking about married life, I asked Ronald if he was seeing anyone. When he said no, I asked him, "When was the last time you had a girlfriend?" "Ten years ago," he replied, and the whole table gasped. None of them knew this about him even though they saw each other frequently at family gatherings.

I was shocked as well, but I took care not to show it. "What's your thinking about that?" was my next question for Ronald. Sometimes I feel like a counselor. I was genuinely interested in why this lovely man had gone so long without someone serious in his life. He answered that he was nearly fifty and felt he was too old to start a family. Since he'd missed the boat, he decided not to bother dating. I then shared with him my own story of recently marrying someone close to his age. Age need not be a barrier to happiness, and of course there are other reasons to have love in your life besides raising a family! I encouraged him not to give up, and of course I started thinking about who might be right for him. The next day, one of the cousins reached out and said, "You managed to find out more about Ronald in one lunch than the rest of us knew from seeing him every month!" It's all about how (and why) you ask.

So be inquisitive, even nosy. You can ask seemingly outrageous things if you do it with humor and some panache. I am a bit of a nosy parker, but people almost always answer my questions—

and enjoy doing so. My formula is simple: When someone trails off out of a sense of decorum, I smile and lean forward with a twinkle, saying, "Sounds like there's a good story behind that. I'd love to hear it." Then I wait. Sometimes there is a silence as the person decides whether to confide, but they almost always do. More often than you think, people are happy to share. You just need to ask. Once they have shared something personal with you, the two of you will feel closer because your relationship will have moved beyond the superficial.

Go Fishing

A question my students frequently ask is how to become closer to someone during a brief interaction. How to maximize time spent together, so that they leave thinking highly of you and wanting to see you again or do business with you. Making someone like you is like fishing—you need to attract. You can't chase or you'll scare away your catch. Instead, use charm to lure them in. Put the bait out there, but wait for your target to bite. The bait is what you have to offer someone. It can be as obvious as resources—knowing their needs and providing a means of filling them. Or it can be as subtle as setting the other person at ease and making them feel that you respect them. All these things will draw someone closer to you.

I attended a party not long ago where one of the other guests was a famous actor. Along with everyone else there, I wanted to meet her, but I didn't want to be too obvious about it. At one point I found myself standing next to her at the buffet table. She was very pregnant, so I asked when her baby was due. "Ah, a Capricorn!" I said. "Yes," she replied, "so is my husband." "Famously great husband material," I replied, smiling. We drifted to different parts of the room. To continue the fishing metaphor, you don't reel in the fish while it's swimming away or the line will break! (Besides, it's good manners to show equal attention to everyone at a gathering rather than just focusing on a select one or two people.)

Later in the evening, I heard her complaining that she had begun having terrible lower back issues so I said, "I couldn't help overhearing. My chiropractor is an absolute miracle worker. Would you like his name?" She took me up on it and texted to thank me about how much he had helped her.

Fishing is about making a good impression in a short amount of time and leaving them wanting more. Be authentic and genuine, and you'll reel them in! If you show interest and someone thinks you like them, they will (almost automatically) like you back. They will, at the very least, admire your good taste.

Manage Expectations

Reading the air is useful in assessing the expectations of others, but as you expand your social circle, it's important to learn how to manage those expectations. Compare what others want with what you're willing to give, and arrive at a (mental) compromise. Skillfully managing expectations will enable you not only to establish healthy boundaries, but also to renegotiate them when necessary, thereby avoiding misunderstandings and creating mutual trust.

It sounds more complicated than it is, and there are those to whom it comes naturally. I got one of my earliest lessons from my high school friend Flora, who was extremely kind but also expert at managing expectations. I remember that I was late one day getting to the dining hall at boarding school. I had recently arrived from Hong Kong, and Flora was one of the few people I knew, so I was delighted to see her sitting in the nearly deserted cafeteria. I walked toward her with my tray, but before I even sat down, she motioned to the open textbook in front of her with an apologetic smile. "I'm studying for an exam next period. I'm afraid I won't be very good company, but I'd still be very happy if you'd sit with me." Letting me know that she wouldn't be able to make conversation while reassuring me that she'd be happy to have my company was clever as well as kind, and it stuck with me.

Avoid the #1 Etiquette Error

Failing to introduce people properly is something I see in social situations again and again. I can't tell you how distressing it is as an etiquette teacher to see how often people fail to make proper introductions. Luckily, just as there's a simple rule about silverware (work your way toward the plate from the outside in), there's a simple rule for introductions. Turn to the more important person first. (For example, "Senator, I'd like to introduce my classmate Gloria," or simply, "Senator, this is my classmate Gloria." Don't say, "Senator, I'd like you to meet my classmate Gloria." That gets the order backward. Just trust me on this one.)

You're showing deference to the person *to whom* you're making the introduction. In the case of equals, you introduce the person you know better to the person you know less well (thereby showing deference to the newcomer).

Here are some examples to help you.

Sample Introductions

Your child's teacher and your father:
"Mrs. Park, I'd like to introduce my father, Mr. Parento." Implicit here is the phrase "to you." That will help you to remember the correct order of the introduction. In this case, what determines the order is not the parties' relative importance but your level of familiarity with them. You know your father better than your child's teacher, so you introduce your father *to* her. Also, when in doubt, introduce men to women. Yes, it's old-fashioned, but so is a lot of traditional etiquette.

Your aunt and your date:
"Aunt Trudy, I'd like to introduce Jon." In the case of your aunt and your date, it is a question of respect for the older generation rather than familiarity. You introduce your date *to* your aunt.

The CEO and the sales rep:
In business, turn to the person with more authority (or higher up in the hierarchy) first and present the person with less authority *to* them. Gender has no place in business etiquette. Also, the client is always given priority.

Two colleagues on the same level:
When introducing two peers to each other, the rule is that you turn to the one you know less well first and introduce your more familiar colleague to them.

A close friend and a new friend:
Introduce your closer friend *to* the person you know less well.
Also, always defer to the person from out of town.

Don't assume two people will start talking just because they are standing or sitting next to each other. And always make sure you accompany the introduction with enough information for them to continue the conversation once you move on. Find at least one subject for them to discuss, such as how they know the host or some common interests between them.

A friend of mine, Leonard, owns an art gallery and invited me for a tour of his new exhibition followed by a seated dinner. I arrived to find half a dozen guests already standing in the entrance of his gallery, staring silently at the art on the walls. I looked around with a smile to see if there was anyone I recognized. There wasn't, but I didn't mind.

Leonard came over to greet me, and we proceeded to have a five-minute conversation. His other guests were left hanging, scattered around the room. One or two were in conversation with each other. Only when I looked expectantly around the room and said, "Who are the other guests here today?" did Leonard bestir himself to introduce me to another guest. He feebly motioned for a friend of his to come over and said, "This is Joe." Then he fell quiet. Everyone felt uncomfortable, including Leonard, but here is what I wish I could have told him: Whether you are a host or a guest, it is important to know how to make introductions. At any gathering, we're forming a community, and it's our responsibility to make each member feel at home quickly. As a host, you need to quickly let each new guest meet as many other guests as possible, so that they feel a sense of belonging, and as a guest, you should also participate in making introductions between other guests.

Make a self-introduction, usually after eye contact and a smile. I like to say, "Hi, I'm Sara. How do you know the host?" And after striking up a conversation with this new friend, you can introduce them to someone else at the party—"Have you met Sally? She is an artist whom Leonard represents."

Put Your Foot Down with a Smile, and Let Someone Else Do the Dirty Work

I threw a celebratory cocktail party for the Netflix debut of *Mind Your Manners* for friends and family in Hong Kong. I invited my eighty-six-year-old grandmother and didn't want her to feel left out, so I pulled aside my friend Howard and asked, "Can you tell my granny about your vineyards in Bordeaux? She loves to drink wine." Out of the dozens of friends there, I chose him because he was just the kind of person who would be engaging and respectful, and know how to impress older people. What's more, I gave him the opportunity to talk about his love for wine and share pictures of his beautiful vineyards. Throughout the evening, I tasked a round-robin of guests with entertaining my grandmother, giving them each about seven minutes with her—long enough to make an impression, short enough to let them continue mingling!

On the other hand, a hostess must sometimes be an enforcer. At the same event, which I threw at a private members' club, a woman who was known to the staff for crashing parties jumped into the elevator and forced her way up. I had been warned about

23

her, so when she said, "Oh you must be Sara! My friend Alan is here so I am just going to find him!" I smiled and replied, "I'm sorry, this is a private party. Alan didn't tell me he was bringing a plus-one." She persisted, saying, "I'm just going over there, just right over there." I stood firm, the smile never leaving my face, and repeated sweetly, "I'm sorry, this is a private party." Then I locked eyes with a staff member across the room who proceeded to usher her out. Remember to put your foot down with a smile, and let someone else do the dirty work.

The same is true when you are on a plane or at a restaurant and another guest is behaving out of order. China banned indoor smoking in 2011, and when I moved to Beijing in 2012 I thoroughly enjoyed the "secondhand" enforcement of this law against secondhand smoke. Whenever the smell of smoke wafted over, I would call over a figure of authority—like the server—and discreetly ask them to ask the guilty party to stop smoking, rather than confront the person myself. Interestingly enough, when it comes to noise pollution, Chinese people are not bothered by loud conversations or phone audio of those sitting near them—very different from, say, Europeans, who respect public space. In an enclosed setting such as an airplane, there is inevitably the gentleman sitting nearby playing games on his phone at maximum volume for the whole cabin to hear. I never hesitate to call the flight attendant and quietly ask them to handle the matter.

Conflicting Engagements

Once you start getting out more, conflicts invariably arise that require tact and finesse. Luckily, that's what etiquette is for. If there's a sticky situation, a rule already exists for how to deal with it. Here are a couple of the most common dilemmas I'm asked about:

1. Stressing about declining invitations

If you have followed the steps in the chapter so far, you might find yourself in this enviable position, but that doesn't mean it won't be uncomfortable sometimes. After all, you have finite time and energy. You want to say no but leave people feeling appreciated and loved rather than rejected. Frame your response so it seems to be all about benefiting them: "Sadly I came down with something, and the last thing I want to do is cough and sneeze all over your guests." This is also an excellent excuse for a last-minute cancellation.

2. Hosting a visitor who hasn't been invited to an event that you were planning to attend

Send a message to the host asking, "By the way, a close friend of mine is staying with me this week and I wanted to ask if it's all right that I bring her with me to your dinner party. I haven't asked her yet, and understand I am imposing, so if it's not convenient I can absolutely come alone." Informing your host that you haven't yet told your friend about the event means you're not putting them in a corner.

If you can't bring your friend, then you can only tell them the truth. ("I have an existing commitment and tried to ask if I could bring you, but they don't have any space. Are you okay with being on your own tonight? Do you want me to give you some suggestions of places to go?") What I've done in the past is arrange, if the guest is from out of town and new to the area, for a local friend to go out with them while I am busy. That way they still have a full agenda and aren't alone.

Assuming your host graciously invites your friend to join, remember when you arrive at the party to immediately greet the host, introduce your friend, and give both a few compliments when making introductions. Talk up your guest to make your host feel honored to have them. Likewise, compliment the host for being so gracious as to allow you to bring your friend.

Finally, if your guest is very important or you feel uncomfortable going to the party without them, send the host a message declining the invitation and explaining your reason for doing so: "I'm very sorry but a friend is staying with me whom I cannot leave alone at home. I hope for us to get together another time." If your host has the space and still wants you to come, they will happily extend the invitation to your guest.

Treat Gossip Like Social Currency

Gossip gets a bad name, but it's also an undeniably useful tool of social bonding. When someone shares a piece of gossip with you, they're handing over a piece of contraband. For that moment at least, you're colluding together. Because in order to qualify as gossip, information has to be negative at the very least, and preferably scandalous. Praising someone behind their back might make us feel virtuous, but it hardly gives us a thrill.

The problem with gossip is that it's a classic driver/pedestrian problem. Say you're driving down a city street and a pedestrian crosses against the light while reading their phone. You slam on your brakes and curse out all pedestrians for being such idiots. Then you park and step into the street without looking. When a car barely misses you, you're instantly furious about reckless drivers. It never occurs to you that a moment ago the positions were reversed. It's the same with gossip. It is precisely as humiliating to be the butt of rumors that may or may not be true as it is delicious to share rumors about someone else's indiscretions.

Which is not to say that people are going to stop gossiping anytime soon. This behavior has been going on for as long as humans have had tongues. But it's very important to discern with whom you choose to share gossip. For example, don't make the mistake of gossiping about someone you don't know very well to someone who knows them better. And don't forget who told you what! A friend of mine recently repeated a very juicy piece of gossip back to the person who had sworn her to secrecy when she had shared it with her originally, thereby ensuring she would never be trusted again. If you get a reputation as a gossip, people will feel they can no longer confide in you or share things with you.

Gossip is social currency, hidden knowledge that gives you power if used properly. The most important thing to establish is context. You need to determine where your loyalties lie. If someone is a close friend, you should be as silent as the tomb with what they share with you. There is a sacred bond between close friends, and to violate that would be a betrayal. Likewise if you are staying with someone and inadvertently discover something about their home life. They have offered you hospitality and there is an ancient code of honor that says guests should not

27

violate the privacy of their hosts. If a terrible secret is burning a hole in your pocket (currency, remember) and sharing it will eat at your conscience, reveal it to someone outside your circle. A final word to the wise: don't trust people who break these rules when telling you other people's secrets.

Kill Them with Kindness

There is one creative solution to the problem of dealing with unpleasant people, short of never leaving home: kill them with kindness. Some people think this means being truly nice. It does not. It means, according to Merriam-Webster, "to cause discomfort to someone by treating him or her in a way that is extremely kind or helpful." The key word here is discomfort. If you are rude, you will be playing right into the other person's hands. They will congratulate themselves on having gotten to you. On the other hand, if you are charming and courteous, you will make them squirm (at least inwardly). It's clear which path is the correct one.

I often say that etiquette is about making others comfortable, but in dealing with rude people our goal is to make them uncomfortable while not appearing to do so. In etiquette, appearances are everything. What is important is not being good but looking good.

When someone treats you rudely, etiquette provides ways of "turning the other cheek" that just so happen to make the other person look bad. It is incredibly satisfying. You get the warm glow of behaving well and the wicked pleasure of holding up a mirror to the other person's behavior. It makes you wonder why everyone doesn't do it.

Your greatest weapon if you dislike someone so intensely you wish they would disappear from the face of the earth is to pretend that it has already happened. If they are in your face and others are watching, dispatch them with a quick, bright "hello" and then busy yourself with something or someone else. Otherwise, ignore completely.

Responding to Rudeness

If someone you don't know well or care about says something rude to you, play deaf. That puts the person in the awkward position of deciding whether to repeat their offensive remark. Even the rudest people don't usually have the gall to do this, but if they do, unnerve them by being charming and courteous in response.

Try this tip the next time a friend makes a joke at your expense or playfully teases you in a way that crosses the line. Pause for a second, look at them, and say, "Are you okay?" It's important that your question comes (or at least appears to come) from a place of care, as if their being a bit "off" were the only possible explanation for saying such a thing. It puts the focus back on them, and at the very least, it will make them think about why they said what they did. Often, they will be embarrassed into an apology. (If they manage to sputter, "Of course I'm okay. Why would you ask that?" your reply can be a Mona Lisa smile and a raised eyebrow.)

Inevitably, there will be people who rub you the wrong way and vice versa. Maybe the two of you had an early misunderstanding, or it could just be bad chemistry. Possibly the person is the new girlfriend of an ex or some such thing. In any case, such hostilities can take on a life of their own. You dread seeing the person. Knowing they will be at an event can make your stomach twist in knots.

That was how it happened with a girl I knew called Becky. She and I disliked each other for years, but neither of us had ever done anything specific to cause it. We did bitch about each other to close friends, however, as I discovered from one of them. I thought Becky was a huge fraud, and people who had worked with her confirmed it. She probably thought I was full of myself. When we saw each other, we would exchange a forced hello and turn away from one another as quickly as we could.

Then one summer we bumped into each other at three gatherings within a month. The first was a pool party, and we exchanged a few courtesies but largely avoided each other. The second was a week later at a restaurant, where we were sitting at different tables, but our groups had overlapping friends. We acted friendly (she went first by saying, "The last time I saw you, we were in bikinis!") and chatted briefly. I introduced her to some people she hadn't yet met at my table, because even though I disliked her, it was the polite thing to do. The third time, shortly thereafter, we were both invited to a friend's house for dinner. I said hello; she peered closely at me and said, "Your skin is so good, why is that? What do you use?" and I replied, "Your skin is good too!" She said, "Oh no, I hate these two lines from my nose to my mouth, and they're just getting deeper." Then we launched into a girl chat on beauty, which led to sharing about everything else in our lives. And of the dozen people there, we ended up hanging out and enjoying each other's company the most. We even left at the same time, and she walked me home and invited me to her birthday party the following weekend.

It was a total surprise that we ended up liking each other. She disarmed me by complimenting me. I reciprocated, and our mutual dislike and wariness evaporated. Sometimes if you pretend to like the other person, it ends up being true. In the absence of real evidence for enmity, keeping an open mind is always a good idea. It's always better to have positive than negative energy in your life.

Practice Etiquette Jujitsu

I often say that etiquette is the glue that holds society together, but etiquette is not all about making others comfortable. The unfortunate truth about human nature is that even nice people are not always nice. We need the tools of etiquette to navigate uncomfortable situations while preserving the facade of civilization, and the best tools give us the power to protect ourselves while escaping or changing those situations. No more suffering in silence!

Some of these situations are relatively innocuous. Let's say I've been cornered by a bore at a party. Do I fret about how to get away without offending? Absolutely not. I simply pair the offender up with another person in the room and drift away with a playful smile.

Use this foolproof trick if you are conversing one-on-one with a perfectly nice person and you just want to get away to mingle. Wait until they seem to have finished a sentence and then jump in, repeating a version of their last sentence and opining on it (e.g., "Yes, you're right, everybody is so accustomed to working from home these days. It's hard to even imagine going back to the office."). This "mirroring" technique serves to wrap up the conversation. Then, without pausing to let them respond, immediately follow up with the exit line of your choice. My favorite is, "I was just on my way to get a new drink. I'll be right back." Then don't return.

My favorite "mirroring" tool to use when others misbehave is etiquette jujitsu. Jujitsu is a martial art that harnesses an opponent's force and uses it against them. When correcting someone's bad behavior, it's clever to build empathy by initially pretending to be on their side. Recently, I hosted a guest who drank much more than was good for him. He was belligerently insisting on having more alcohol, and his girlfriend was pleading with him to drink water instead. Everyone except the drunk man was getting embarrassed. I approached him and began laughing in a playful way. "You can have another drink," I said, "but first you need to take a shot of water." Then I plunked a huge glass of water on the table in front of him and dared him to chug it. By speaking his language and using humor to disguise my motives, I succeeded in distracting him from the liquor bottle. A few minutes later, his girlfriend was able to persuade him to go home.

Etiquette jujitsu works particularly well in brief verbal inter-actions. I'm often asked, for example, if I have any advice about how to deal with name-droppers and bluffers. For a foolproof way to shut them up, flip the script and say, "Wow! You know so many famous people! When are you going to introduce us to Nicole Kidman?"

I was impressed by how one of my best friends recently han-dled an acquaintance who happens to be a huge name-dropper and social climber. At a party at the end of summer, he made a beeline for her and immediately boasted, "I just came back from Saint-Tropez, Mykonos, Sardinia, and Ibiza. How was your sum-mer?" She looked him in the eye and said in a deadpan voice, "Same cities, different order." Ouch.

FRIENDS

If social life is the sundae, friends are the cherry on top. The word "friendship" covers a vast spectrum of intimacy, from mere acquaintances to those we consider members of our chosen family. There are friendships of convenience, of proximity, and of shared interest, but true friendships are purely voluntary. Unlike our other relationships, whether family, work, or romantic, true friendships have no reason for existing but themselves. That's what makes them so beautiful.

Though we may view our relationships with friends as informal, there is a delicate dance that must be navigated, further complicated by the absence of the "rulebook" that exists for dating and the workplace. Daily situations arise that demand judgment and tact to avoid hurt feelings and missteps. And while some people possess a natural talent for friendship, an innate understanding of how to conduct themselves in every circumstance, the rest of us must learn.

Friend or Faux?

First, let's define our terms. In the era of social media, the word "friend" is more liable to be obscure than clear. By lumping together many different relationships under a single label, we run the risk of treating people similarly even when they play different roles in our lives. As the renowned British anthropologist Robin Dunbar discovered, the average person has about five hundred acquaintances, yet our inner circle consists of only five loved ones, followed by fifteen good friends, fifty friends, and 150 meaningful contacts. To mistake our contacts and acquaintances for friends is to invite trouble. So when it comes to friendship, context is of the utmost importance.

True Politeness Is the Art of Choosing Among One's Real Thoughts

Every now and then I'll come across someone who tells me, "Oh, I have no etiquette. I'm too honest to have good etiquette!" This belief is based on a gross misunderstanding of etiquette, which does not require that you lie (although you certainly can "lie from the heart" if necessary to spare someone's feelings, depending on the context). Etiquette asks only that you speak and act kindly. In the immortal words of Judith Martin, "If you can't be kind, at least be vague."

I am not advocating for dishonesty, or at least, not exactly. True politeness is the art of choosing among one's real thoughts. As in an interview, answer the question you want to answer, not the one that is asked. For example, if your host at a dinner party inquires about the food and it tastes deplorable, you can dodge a straight answer by saying, "What a beautiful presentation," or "How did you manage to get tomatoes out of season?"

I had occasion to use this advice recently when I visited my husband's hometown of Lishui in Zhejiang province. Lishui, which means "beautiful waters," is known as one of the most eco-friendly cities in China and home to some of the cleanest air and freshest produce; nearly every dish presented to me in Lishui was delicious. The Chinese banquets we attended there were some of the most exquisite meals I have eaten in my life. Then one day, we were invited to dinner at a new restaurant, opened by a friend of a friend. The meal was terrible. My husband could tell what I was thinking, because I only ate from one of the dozen dishes, which was a fish head soup. The hostess asked me how I liked the food. "This fish head soup is the best dish here," I replied emphatically.

Unlike acquaintances, real friends are entitled to your honest opinion. Though it may be painful in the moment, you are saving them from the secret judgment of others. To prioritize your comfort over a friend's by failing to point out an obvious flaw is to do them a great disservice.

This reminds me of a group of neighbors with whom I often share potluck dinners. On three occasions, my friend Kimberly prepared a dish in which I found a hair. The first and second times, I discreetly left the hair untouched on my plate and said nothing. But on the third occurrence, I knew I had to speak up. The most important thing was not to do it in front of other people. That would make her lose face, which was the opposite of what I was trying to do.

I waited until we were walking alone the following week and said, "By the way, I found a hair in the last dish you brought. I used to have the same issue until I started wearing a hairband when I cook." (Not true, but it was a good way to soften the blow.) Then I subtly eased out of the topic by complimenting her on the eggplant dish she'd brought and asking her for the recipe. This lightened the focus on her embarrassment before I changed the subject completely.

> Being careless about the distinction between friends and acquaintances can cause problems. Err in one direction and you will cause offense by being too free with your opinions and advice. Err in the other, and you will end up sharing information with those who should not have it.

With extremely close friends, you can speak your mind freely even when giving advice that may be hard to hear, always being mindful of your audience. I have such a friend in Olivier. He is from Paris, exceedingly direct and confrontational, and he has kept me in check several times when I've misbehaved or said something inappropriate.

A couple years ago, I hosted a dozen friends for afternoon drinks in my garden. I was too lazy to change out of my tight bike shorts from grocery shopping earlier in the day, but had changed my sporty top for a summer sweater. Five minutes after guests began to arrive, Olivier beckoned me into a corner and hissed, "What on earth are you wearing? You're a hostess, but you look like you're going to the gym! And those bike shorts are so tight you have a massive camel toe! Go and put on some proper clothes right now!" I immediately went and changed my attire. Though it was jarring to hear the truth, I was grateful to him for telling me what others would no doubt be thinking.

A friend who will be honest with you, even if it means wounding you with love, is priceless. Right after college, my close friend John was dumped by his three-year girlfriend. He spent months complaining and moaning every time we spoke on the phone. At the six-month mark, I decided enough was enough. "John, I love you like a brother," I told him, "and I will always be here for you when you need me. But it's been half a year. Are you really going to just mope and wallow, or are you going to pick yourself back up and do something with your life?" There was a long pause. To my surprise, he said, "You're right. I'm going to change my mindset and do something about this." The next day he set up a few online dating profiles and thanked me for the loving kick to get him back into action.

Even with close friends, however, there are boundaries that need to be respected, and the key is to know when to push and when to back off. People have varying capacities for intimacy, and even within the same friendship someone can have different ideas than you of what is acceptable to share.

It's important even with our dear friends to know how to rebuff gently if they have overstepped. Selective deafness, vagueness, and a deft change of topic are always good choices. If those don't work (with close friends, after all, they might not) you can deflect with cheeky humor or a sheepish smile and say, "That's private." It's equally important to learn how to accept a rebuff with grace. If you're going to be curious and press for information, you need to accept the possibility of being told you've crossed a line. Retreat with grace.

(You Gotta Be) Cruel to Be Kind

What about sharing uncomfortable truths when the context is unclear? Etiquette is about saving ourselves and others from discomfort and embarrassment, but there are occasions when we need to be "cruel to be kind." In other words, when we have to embarrass someone (briefly) to save them from greater embarrassment. Say someone has spinach stuck in her teeth. Yes, she might feel a quick sting of embarrassment if you point it out, but she'll be grateful you did. It's preferable to going around like that until she discovers it for herself and painfully replays how many times she's smiled since she finished that salad. It's easy to use etiquette as an excuse to let ourselves off the hook from delivering distressing truths, even when it's the right thing to do. In weighing context and courtesy, think about whether you'd want someone to do the same for you.

One of the most common questions I receive as an etiquette teacher is how to address body odor or bad breath. Interestingly, there are cultural variances at work here. In China, we are more likely to state uncomfortable truths openly. Upon seeing someone after an absence, it is perfectly normal to remark that they've gained weight, for example, or that their skin has broken out. It's even considered a sign of caring. In the US, on the other hand, only positive comments are considered acceptable. Remarking on personal hygiene issues in America, where "cleanliness is next to godliness," is very tricky. Context is crucial when balancing the reward of helping someone against the risk of irreparably harming your relationship.

If you must, in the case of someone you don't know well but see often, you could try saying, "A good friend of mine told me about this great deodorant she found that I've been using. She used to have body odor and nothing else worked. Do you want the name of it?" If you need to take it a step further, you could say, "Oh, I think I smell something—is that your BO or mine?" Then take a subtle whiff of your own armpits and add, "I just tried this deodorant that my friend recommended and I'm not sure if it's working." Making it an "us" thing rather than a "them" thing allows them to save face.

> If someone near you offers you a piece of gum or a mint, take it.

A Case Study in Saving Face

My favorite etiquette anecdote, often called the Silver Salt Shaker effect, is a case study in saving face. The story goes that Winston Churchill was having dinner at an English manor with fellow dignitaries. Looking across the table, he saw a guest slip a priceless silver salt shaker into his pocket. He spent the rest of the meal trying to figure out how he was going to get it back without causing a scene and embarrassing his hosts. Then he had an "aha" moment. He put the matching pepper shaker into his own pocket. When it was time to leave, he walked over to the thief and stealthily revealed the pepper shaker. "We've been spotted," Churchill told him with a guilty smile. "I think we should return them." The moral of the story? You should always give someone a way to save face, even if it takes a little creativity. We have a saying in Chinese that is a corollary to this principle. You should always offer someone a *tai jie*, which means a flight of stairs, to come down. It means providing someone with a graceful way out of a tricky situation, such as room to say no without giving offense. The kernel of truth here is that no matter what culture you're in, never back someone into a corner. If you absolutely must confront them, do it innocently and delicately. People can become truly vicious when they have no options and nothing to lose.

Saving and losing face (*mianzi*) is a Chinese concept. Losing face is a serious matter, and it has been estimated that there are 113 Chinese terms for different shades of shame. Confucius, who laid the foundation for much of Chinese culture 2,500 years ago, considered shame a virtue and promoted "a sense of shame" because it was more effective than laws in maintaining a harmonious society. Laws were only necessary for outcasts and troublemakers. The Chinese carving above Boston's Chinatown, which greeted arriving immigrants, read, "Propriety, Righteousness, Integrity, and a Sense of Shame."

Cultural anthropologists distinguish between "guilt cultures" like the US (which emphasize internal conscience) and "shame cultures" like Japan, Korea, and China (which underscore how behavior looks to outsiders). Guilt keeps people in line in America much as shame does in these Asian societies. It is an oversimplification to say that any culture has a monopoly on either guilt or shame, but the difference is that shame in Asian cultures is relationship oriented. It is about how your actions reflect not only on you but on those in your family and social circle.

So what do traditional "shame cultures" have in common with the current online "shaming culture"? The answer is very little. Asian shame cultures are based on honor. Shaming culture is based on *humiliation*, which is the deliberate infliction of shame. This is not to say that public shaming is entirely new. It has evolved over

42

time, changing venues as society has changed. In the past, it took place in town squares. Now it occurs primarily online, where social media posts make it easy to quickly generate mass outrage by encouraging impulsive attacks and group piling-on. What "shaming" induces is fear, rather than the desire to do better.

The Friend Who Got Away

We all have one—the friend who got away. Every time you think of them it hurts, and somehow the pain never lessens. Our society conditions us to expect that romantic relationships will end, so we're taught how to deal with that. There are shoulders to cry on, books to read, ways to cushion the pain of loss—but there is no training or preparation for losing a friend. We expect our close friendships to last forever, perhaps because sex isn't clouding our judgment. But the process of getting close to a friend can feel very much like falling in love. And that's where the trouble comes in.

> There is a Chinese proverb that says, "Friendships between gentlemen are as calm as water, while those between petty men are sweet as new wine." What it means is that long-lived friendships are clear and transparent, maintaining emotional equilibrium despite their closeness. Inferior friendships, which lack boundaries, are vulnerable to bickering and drama. They are cloying, like sweet wine, and destined to fail.

It's all very well to theorize about these matters, but that doesn't diminish the hurt and betrayal we feel when it happens.

My "friend who got away" was Deirdre, whom I met in college. We were so close she was almost like the sister I never had, and it never occurred to me that our friendship wouldn't last. When I moved to New York to work as an analyst at the boutique investment bank Perella Weinberg, she accepted a job in the city as well, and we spent a wonderful year working hard and playing hard. But then I moved to Beijing, and it became more difficult to stay in touch. When I visited New York, I still stayed at her apartment, but then she started dating someone I thought was a terrible person. Her job took her all over the world and it was hard to keep track of her. Once or twice, I saved the wrong number for her in a new phone, so my calls and messages to her failed to go through. I thought she hadn't replied, while she thought I never reached out. Then I founded my etiquette school, which was incredibly time-consuming.

After a year or two of no contact besides an occasional message, I heard through mutual friends that Deirdre had just visited Beijing, and I was confused because usually I would be the first (and sometimes the only) person she would call. When I tried to contact her, though, I received no answer. I double-checked that I had the right number. She had dropped me. It left me confused and sad, but I'm not someone who dwells or is confrontational.

About six years after we last saw each other, I visited New York when I knew Deirdre was in the city and reached out. She replied by text that she was too busy with work to see me, so I sent her this message: "I'm in town and would love to see you. I'm not sure what I did to hurt an old friend, but I would like to at least understand what I did wrong so I could try to make it right." She brushed me off, saying that she was really just busy.

There was nothing left to do but accept it. Though it bothers me to this day, I know that not everyone will be in your life forever.

How to Drop a Friend

There is an etiquette to dropping a friend without drama. I dislike confrontation, but I learned from my experience with Deirdre that I never want to make anyone feel the way I did in that situation. The story of my friend Tanya from Shanghai is a good illustration of the Chinese idiom of "raising the reins and riding your separate ways." I'm busy running my own business, entertaining, and teaching, and I like to see a variety of friends. But when I became friends with Tanya, she wanted to get together all the time. To avoid feeling claustrophobic and missing out on seeing my other friends, I would invite a few others to come along. Very quickly I noticed that Tanya began hanging out exclusively with the friends I had introduced her to. I actually wondered if she had any friends of her own. Of course I wasn't going to ask her because it would sound petty, and it was such a tiny issue it didn't warrant confrontation. Instead, I distanced myself from her so slowly and gradually that she didn't even realize it had happened. She was so attached to the people I had introduced her to that she hardly even noticed I was no longer there.

> "True friends are never apart, maybe in distance but never in heart."
>
> —UNKNOWN

SOCIAL LIFE AND FRIENDSHIP:
DIGITAL ETIQUETTE

How to Be Your Best Self Online

The digital world constitutes a microculture of its own. When we contrast it with IRL, we tacitly acknowledge that it has a life of its own. Social media, texting, even email—each has its own set of rules. Digital natives who grew up speaking these languages might know them intuitively; others need them to be explicitly spelled out. It's beyond the scope of an etiquette book to decode an entire digital microculture, but even those who are fluent could use a few reminders of the principles we sometimes violate even when we know better.

Online Content Slips Out of Context

Etiquette is always concerned with context, but social media poses a unique problem: content migration. A post might be perfectly appropriate in its original context, yet online content has a nasty way of refusing to stay put. What looks perfectly innocuous on your personal feed won't necessarily "read" the same when viewed by a prospective employer. The major selling point of Snapchat was that conversations disappeared as soon as they were sent, neatly avoiding this problem. But for most platforms, once you post something, it might as well be carved in stone. Press send, and it becomes public property.

We make the distinction between online and "real life," but when something from your past (recent or ancient) comes back to haunt you, you realize that life online can be all too real. Don't say or do online what you wouldn't be comfortable saying or doing offline. And since what is shared in one context can be viewed elsewhere, you need to think not only about the current context but also about how your post will translate into the future. Yes, it's depressing, and repressive, but you always have to keep the worst-case scenario in mind when posting, texting, emailing, or (most importantly) sexting. In other words, think about your reputation online as well as off.

A former boss on Wall Street, Terry Meguid, once told me, "A reputation takes a lifetime to build and a second to lose." And the fastest way to lose it is on social media.

Texting Etiquette

You probably know these basic rules of etiquette, but just as with table manners, it doesn't hurt to be reminded . . .

Don't use text to deal with conflict

Pick up the phone or meet face-to-face. Never try to resolve sensitive issues through text messaging—given you can't see each other's facial expressions or hear each other's tone of voice, it's more likely that things will be misinterpreted.

Don't text too late or too early

Although most of us silence our phones when sleeping, you would be surprised by the number who don't. Limit your texting to reasonable waking hours—otherwise shoot off an email!

Don't ask questions that are difficult to answer in one sentence

Texting is for short conversations, not long philosophical dialogues or soul-searching questions. Save those for face-to-face or on the phone. And do not fire off multiple questions in a row, unless you want to successfully scare or annoy someone away.

Keep your texts to about the same length as the other person's

Social interaction should be balanced. Just as you should not monopolize a conversation face-to-face, you should not type essays to someone who replies with a couple of words, and vice versa. Keep your word count to the same amount.

A Note on Voice Notes

Voice notes—sometimes called voice texts or voice messages—are short audio recordings available in many messaging apps. They are gaining in popularity because they combine the ease of a text with the human voice's ability to capture nuances of mood, tone, and humor.

Another appealing feature is that they are generally deleted automatically after a short time, depending on the app. Voice messages are considered informal and should not be used in a business context.

Social Media 101

Posting
There's no such thing as posting too little or too often—content is key. Interesting and engaging content will attract people, but boring content will turn people away. Don't post just to post!

Tagging
If you tag one, then tag them all. And never tag someone who is not in the photo.

Reposting
If you are reposting someone else's content, tag the source.

Posting photos without permission
This depends on the level of your friendship with others in the photo, the type of event, and the type of photos. If it was a conference, then everybody has the expectation that photos will be posted. But perhaps your friend cares about her public image on social media and would want to photoshop out her eyebags. Go with your gut—if you are even the slightest bit unsure, then ask for permission first.

Avoiding too many hashtags
According to a recent study, three to five hashtags is the right number. More and you look like you're trying too hard. Too few and you're missing out on reach.

Separating business and personal content

Some people have two accounts (a private one for friends and a public one for business) while others choose not to post overly personal content on their social media. It's up to you, really.

Curbing self-promotion

Your friends and followers want to be entertained, inspired, and informed on social media, just as they do in real life. They don't want to be advertised to. It's a fine balance. Don't overdo it.

Responding to negative comments

Even the most popular celebrities will get hate. So long as someone likes you, there will be someone who dislikes you—this is the principle of yin and yang. So the best response is no response. Don't give energy to it!

Friending people you don't know

It's okay to friend someone you haven't yet met if you have a compelling reason for doing so. Perhaps you have mutual friends and you want to use their business services. Plenty of relationships (of all sorts) have begun online . . .

Sliding into someone's DMs

Go ahead, as long as you're being safe and respectful, and not creepy. You don't have much to lose besides a little pride.

Digital Boundary Setting

Much of etiquette has to do with setting and respecting boundaries, and digital boundary setting begins with physical boundaries.

If you're in the presence of someone with a heartbeat, prioritize their feelings. There's nothing more annoying or potentially hurtful than trying to have a face-to-face conversation with someone who is focused on their screen or constantly checking to see if they have any messages. (One of the most common deal-breakers on first dates is someone continually checking their phone.) If you're expecting an important call or message, tell the person you're with in advance and apologize for the possible interruption.

Next are the boundaries we set with ourselves and our devices. Almost all of us are digital addicts to some degree. Our brains need the dopamine hit we get from checking our phones, and they are going to manipulate our behavior to get it. Still, pride and common sense must prevail to some degree. Repeat after me: mute, unfollow, unplug. Mute, Unfollow, Unplug.

> Whether you decide not to look at your phone in the morning until you've gone outside for a few minutes (a guaranteed happiness-booster), turn off your notifications while working or dining with friends and family, or use an app to limit your screen time, it's good for your social ties, your productivity, and your character to set some boundaries.

Finally, there are the boundaries we set with others online. Just because we are technically available twenty-four hours a day doesn't mean we should be. Most relationships will not benefit from that kind of unlimited access. But people won't know what our limits are unless we communicate them, either outright or in a more subtle way. Managing expectations, described earlier in this chapter, pertains just as much or more to life online as to IRL. Whether we're talking about friends, lovers, colleagues, or family, decide early in the relationship when and how quickly you want or need to reply. People become conditioned as to what to expect. Don't respond late at night, for example, if you don't want to convey availability at that hour. Boundaries can change, but they need to remain comfortable for both sides.

Group Chats

Most people love and rely on a group chat of three to four intimate friends, but I think we can all agree that it's time for the mass group chat to die a quick and painful death. In the meantime, here are some ground rules for chats of all sizes.

What NOT to do in group chats

1. **Do not spam the group chat:** Nobody wants to be spammed, especially with photos of your dog or cat—or kids. Check your fake news before sharing it. And don't text-vomit (you know what I mean).

2. **What happens in the group chat stays in the group chat:** Do not forward photos or personal information, and especially do not screenshot someone else's comments without permission. Group chats should be safe spaces, even if nobody has explicitly said so.

3. **Do not add new people without asking current members first:** Your chat group is like a private party. It's rude to pull new people into the chat without asking

existing members first—unless you are the host of a group chat and have a good reason (you're a gym owner and the chat group consists of willing, subscribed clients). When you do add a new person, be sure to make a proper introduction, like you would in real life.

4. **Do not have a one-on-one conversation with another member:** Subjecting others in the group chat to a bombardment of messages between you and another person is bad manners. It is selfishly taking up screen space. If the dialogue turns into a public fight, the only one who will regret it is you. Message someone directly if what you want to say isn't for the group.

5. **Try not to take it personally if your post is ignored:** The possibilities for hurt feelings are exponentially multiplied in this setting. Oftentimes people get caught up in their day and forget to reply.

6. **Do not be overreactive, rude, or hurtful:** Everything is magnified on screen, and dry humor can easily be misinterpreted for the worse without your smile to soften it. Even more than you would in person, hold your tongue and keep any extreme judgments to yourself.

7. **Go light on emojis, symbols, and punctuation:** This is not the time to show your enthusiasm. In fact, these should be curbed for all online conversations.

SOCIAL LIFE AND FRIENDSHIP: FAQ

At what point in a conversation with a person you've just met is it polite to ask what they do for a living (if at all)?

I have met people who care more about a person's occupation than their actual name! It must appear to enter the conversation naturally, even if you deliberately steer it that way. Make at least ten minutes of small talk before asking innocently, "What sort of work brings you to Miami?"

When someone new asks me what I do for work, should I ask them as well after answering?

Absolutely. It would be impolite not to. Returning the question is an excellent opportunity to find out more about someone. Just say, "And how about you?"

When giving hugs for greetings, should you hug again when leaving?

No matter the custom, make a ceremony out of leaving. It can be a handshake or a hug or a kiss, but if you don't say a proper goodbye, it's like a sentence hanging with no period at the end

How do you ask where a piece of clothing or purse is from that you admire on someone?
Compliment a detail ("What a unique color . . .") and say, "I've been looking for something like that!" Then just ask. People are flattered that you want to emulate what they're wearing.

A friend was half an hour late to meet me and I left. Should I have stayed?
The last time someone was half an hour late to meet me it was an acquaintance who had asked to meet up for coffee. I looked at my watch when the apologetic offender arrived and said with a big smile, "Don't worry, but I only have fifteen minutes left." The implication? Talk fast.

What's the proper way to react when a friend doesn't show at an appointment? This person asked me for a favor and I rearranged my day to help them. When I arrived at the meeting place, they texted me and said they didn't need me anymore.
Save your energy and drop them. That's bad character, forget bad manners. A friend like that is not a friend worth having.

When someone monopolizes a conversation and doesn't let anyone else get a word in edgewise, how do I stop them without offending?
Interrupt and say, "Ann, that's so interesting! We'll have to hear more another time. Paul, what have you been up to these days?" If Ann tries to monopolize the conversation yet again, jump in and say, "Ann, we've made you speak so much we must let you rest and eat your food."

How do you react when your neighbor at a gathering farts or burps?
Pretend it never happened. This is a good time to practice selective deafness or blindness. On the flip side, if you burp at the table simply say, "Excuse me." If you are the guilty farter, stay silent and quickly leave the offending area.

Is it ever okay to ask who is going to an event before you RSVP?
Never. Although it is acceptable to ask casually after you confirm your attendance ("I'd love to attend . . . Will anyone else I know be there?"), I personally never do it. I treat anyone I bump into as a bonus.

When you invite someone over for a few hours, is it important to show them around your house?
A house tour is not mandatory for guests. Generally speaking, Americans like to give a tour, Europeans don't really, and in Asia people prefer to entertain outside of their homes. One of my favorite scenes from Emily in Paris *is when Emily arrives at her French friend's country estate. She asks for a tour, and the friend's mother says in French, "and does she want a tour of the laundry room too?"*

If it's family or close friends, they are of course curious to see your home, but otherwise you can demur and say something about it being messy or vaguely promise "next time." Even if you do show them around, you don't need to include your bedroom.

How do I deal with people I'm not fond of at a party?
Avoid them. If that's impossible, be pleasant and keep the exchange as brief as you can before you head off to find your friends. Make any excuse to cut the conversation short. I've even turned down invitations upon discovering there will be people present whom I'd rather not see. Better to spend time in your own company than with disagreeable folk.

How do I tactfully leave a party early?
Find a good moment to tell your host in a hushed tone out of earshot of others. Then stay a while longer before slipping out without fanfare. Otherwise, you risk leading all the other guests out the door like the Pied Piper of Hamelin, and you will feel terribly guilty for bringing the party to an untimely end.

What should I do when friends talk about something I don't know anything about and I feel out of my depth?
I've often noticed that secure and confident people are not afraid of showing what they don't know. Not asking is a way to guarantee you'll remain ignorant! However, if it's a big group and everyone besides you seems to know what's going on, don't disrupt the conversational flow just for yourself (that's selfish). Pull the person closest to you aside, and quietly ask them to explain it to you. Otherwise, look it up on your phone later.

My friend bitched about me behind my back. How do I confront her?
You must do it face-to-face, or if necessary over the phone—no texts or emails! Stay calm and repeat back exactly what you heard. If you're lucky, she never said it or her words were taken out of context, in which case you can both be pissed at the person who made up the story. If not, tell her, "I want to understand why you would say that." Then wait to hear whether she deserves your continued friendship.

I uploaded a picture of my friend on social media and she got really upset because she said it was a bad picture of her. Was it wrong of me to upload without asking?
There's a running joke in China that true friends are those who

photoshop others in the picture, instead of just themselves, before posting. I believe there's often truth in humor. Be a true friend.

Is it okay to vent about something or shame someone on social media?

Only if you are prepared to look bitter (never a good look) and for this to come back and bite you (because it almost always does). Play your venting out in your mind, which will give you the mental satisfaction of doing it. Or vent to a friend or colleague nearby. But not in public.

Is it appropriate to post swimsuit photos on social media if your colleagues or boss can see them?

You may think that baring some skin is no big deal, but it's unprofessional to allow your colleagues to see you in a bathing suit. If you must, at least put on a cover-up.

I was scrolling through my socials and discovered I was not invited to an event. How do I raise this?

If it was your best friend's birthday, you can confront her in person—remember to be gentle and approach the conversation from a confused perspective. But in any other situation, too bad. Nobody is obligated to invite you to their party.

Someone suddenly blocked me after a super friendly message. What should I do?

If it is a friend, then it's worth the effort to find out why—although a dramatic friend who jumps to conclusions and will block you without room for explanation is not worth having! If they are simply an acquaintance or somebody you barely know, leave it. Life is too short to spend figuring out other people's issues.

PART TWO

WORK

Mastering others is strength.
Mastering yourself is true power.

—LAO TZU

If you are the smartest person in the room,
then you are in the wrong room.

—CONFUCIUS

Your Best Self at Work

The work world is today's biggest microculture. Whether you're a seasoned veteran or just starting out in your career, there's always more to learn about its complicated social dynamics. Being your best self here calls for a continually shifting balance between being true to yourself and protecting yourself, and what is authentic in a work context is not necessarily synonymous with what is authentic in your personal life. We are experiencing a tectonic generational slide in which the two are starting to overlap, but they are still not the same. The work world is a place in continual transition.

Certain principles like developing "soft skills," decoding the rules of reciprocity, and protecting your boundaries and sanity remain vital to surviving and thriving in this context, no matter where you are in your career trajectory. In this chapter, I share both tools for success and solutions to the most common problems that crop up. Finally, I impart some mildly Machiavellian techniques to help you get ahead. Just because we're nice doesn't mean we're naive!

The Second Secret of Social Fluency: Decode the System

Social fluency depends on reading people and situations with speed as well as accuracy. In order to survive hopping from one culture to another in my early years, I was compelled to develop an almost uncanny ability to decode whatever system I was in—and to do it fast. People make up their minds about you quickly when you are the new kid on the block, and you don't have much time to figure out how to fit in.

As we've read, the first secret of social fluency, reading the air, draws upon an intuitive sense of what's happening in a new environment. The second secret, decoding the system, is far more analytical. It requires donning your anthropologist's hat and identifying who's who and what function they serve within a given structure. In a new school, for example, you must pay attention not only to how your own classmates relate to each other but also to how the classes ahead of you operate, along with the teachers, the administration, and even the founders. What is the school's message, its "ethos," if you will? Knowing this will help you navigate the culture. A large public high school has different goals and social conventions than a charter school, which is different from a boarding school.

When I landed on campus as a fourteen-year-old at the elite American boarding school Phillips Exeter Academy, I was wearing what cool girls wore at the German Swiss International School in Hong Kong: super low-rise, wide-legged jeans, a semi-sheer, midriff-baring Roxy crop top, a choker, four piercings down the helix of my right ear, and a red stripe in my hair. In retrospect, I'm shocked that my parents let me dress this way, when everybody else was dressed straight out of *The Official Preppy Handbook*. There was a school dress code, and boys had to wear a jacket, shirt, and tie. For girls it was looser, but I remember being horrified by what I later learned were Vera Bradley bags, which struck me as totally frumpy.

Within ten days, I took the school shuttle bus to the local shopping mall and replaced most of my wardrobe with pieces from J.Crew, Abercrombie, and Express—and Victoria's Secret. The weekend after, I removed all of my piercings. By the next, I had found myself an Hervé Chapelier two-toned tote. (I could never bring myself to buy a Vera Bradley. A girl's gotta draw the line somewhere.) Some people could criticize me for changing my wardrobe and say I lost my sense of individuality, but I did it because it made me feel more comfortable and others more comfortable around me. I felt like I belonged.

In essence, the clothes were a code. In this case, to the upper middle class in the northeastern United States. Even though no one was ever going to mistake me for a New England prep, I was showing that I respected the culture.

Decoding is not necessarily about discovering the channels of power or influence, but in a hierarchical structure like a company or industry it would be naive not to. Once you figure out where they lie, you can subtly and "naturally" maneuver yourself to the top—if you have the courage to take the initiative.

STARTING OUT

Develop Your "Soft Skills"

Your qualifications might get you an interview, but the great majority of career success comes from having well-developed social or "soft" skills. Also known as people skills or core skills, these are becoming ever more important in the era of remote and hybrid work. Communication, teamwork, openness to criticism, and time management are always in demand.

What to Ask in a Job Interview

Don't be lulled into complacency by the harmless sounding "Do you have any questions for me?" that comes at the end of an interview. Last impressions are lasting impressions. Be prepared. It's better not to ask any questions than to ask stupid questions—and yes, in an interview where you are being judged from the second you step through the door, there is such a thing as a stupid question. Anything that can be found on the company website falls into that category! Focus instead on asking about your interviewer's personal experience:

What do you personally like most about working here?

How would you describe your company's culture?

What have past employees done to succeed in this position?

What am I not asking that I should?

How to Write an Eye-Catching Resume

Your resume is a "first impression on paper" designed to capture a prospective employer's interest quickly. Most employers spend only thirty seconds reviewing a resume, so use your time wisely. For those just starting out, here are some suggestions:

- Keep it to one page.
- Do your homework on the position and the company, and be strategic and intentional about what to include.
- Emphasize only relevant activities and quantify *accomplishments* rather than simply listing responsibilities.
- Avoid passive phrases like "was in charge of" or "responsible for."

- Highlight "soft" skills, which transfer from one context to another.
- Say what you did, not what you were supposed to do.
- Proofread, with close attention to verb tenses.

Final tip: As I told my student Raishel Jones in Episode 3 of *Mind Your Manners*, don't neglect to mention activities and passions pertinent to the job even if they were unpaid.

How to Nail a Cover Letter

A cover letter is used to introduce your resume to a prospective employer. Always send one unless explicitly told not to. Your cover letter is your opportunity to show your interest in the position and why you are an ideal candidate.

Here's how to write the perfect cover letter:

- Always address your cover letter to a specific person and keep it to one page.
- Be enthusiastic and natural, and provide specific examples of your credentials early—you want to give them a reason to interview you.
- Use active verbs and avoid "-ing" endings where possible.
- Avoid cringeworthy expressions like "I am the ideal candidate."
- Proofread, spell-check, and make sure you're sending to the correct person and company, especially if you're sending out lots of resumes.
- Most importantly, be confident: don't apologize for

what you don't have, and don't say you "hope" or "believe" anything—state your credentials and experience with confidence.

- Finally, sign it for a humanizing touch.

Be Brave: "If You Don't Ask, You Don't Get"

If I asked you to guess who said that, I bet you wouldn't come up with Mahatma Gandhi! Often we're afraid to ask for an opportunity, a raise, or a promotion because we fear rejection. But what's the worst that can happen if you don't get what you ask for? Only that you don't get it. You won't *lose* anything by asking, but if you don't ask, the answer will always be no! Internalizing this truth can work wonders for your career and even other areas of your life.

When I was applying to business schools, I had a two-month window to visit different campuses and observe classes. I reached out to colleagues and friends asking if they knew anyone at Harvard, Wharton, or Columbia who could host me. I visited all of the schools, sat in on classes, and then asked my hosts to advise me on the admissions process. When I had submitted my application and was granted an interview at Harvard (which means you have a decent shot at getting accepted), I went online and found their thirty most frequently asked interview questions. I opened up a Word document and wrote out all my answers. Then I reached out to everyone I knew who was already there and asked them to conduct mock interviews with me. I hadn't seen some of them in years, but they happily agreed. They even spent hours helping me vet my final answers.

All this hard work paid off with an acceptance letter, and the first week of orientation I was sitting around with a bunch of fellow classmates comparing application stories. I believed I had over-prepared and "over-connected" to an almost ludicrous degree, but it soon became apparent that everyone else had done exactly the same thing. This is a characteristic behavior of successful people: they ask, and they get.

Recently I received a friendship request on WeChat (China's messenger super app) from a stranger who had added me through the Harvard Business School group chat. In the request, she wrote, "I am HBS class of 2024, and I am exploring my career direction after graduation. Would you have thirty minutes for a video call to share your experience?" What initiative! I messaged her back, "I'll take you out for a proper coffee." She'll go far.

Seek Out Mentors and Role Models, and Pay Back the Favor

A great way to shore up hard and soft skills at once is to find a mentor. The summer before my senior year of college, I did an internship at Morgan Stanley's investment banking division based in Hong Kong. Of all the managing directors, one of the most widely talked about was Deborah Mei. She was head of Asia-Pacific Consumer, Retail, Gaming, and Industrial Investment Banking for Morgan Stanley, the only female managing director at the time. She also had an educational pedigree, was a strikingly beautiful Eurasian woman, and had a fabulous sense of style. Deborah Mei was iconic. When the heads of groups were trotted out to meet and greet us interns during orientation, we eagerly awaited Deborah Mei. She didn't disappoint. When she ended her meet and greet by telling all forty of us that we were welcome to schedule time with her personally, I took her up on it. (She later told me I was the only one who did.)

Pro Tip: You are never too junior to reach out to business contacts to network.

Deborah had attended Phillips Academy Andover and I had attended Phillips Exeter Academy, two boarding schools founded by the same family. That was my starting point for conversation, to lay common ground. Then I peppered her with questions about her career and asked for her advice. In fact, I did this with all the managing directors and heads of groups. And what I observed was that all the most senior bankers had started their careers in New York City, on Wall Street, the world's center of finance. Her advice convinced me that I wanted to do the same.

Three years later, when Deborah moved to Beijing to open the China office of a new boutique investment bank, she reached out to me. I had moved from New York to Beijing at the same time to begin volunteering for a nonprofit, and she needed to recruit a junior banking team. While I had no interest in returning to finance, and told her so, I did send out a mass email with a job description she provided me, and she ended up hiring two of the people I had sent her way. A year later, she returned the favor by writing an outstanding recommendation letter for my business school applications. This was the culmination of my initiative to knock on her door and spend twenty minutes sitting in her office. I learned that you never know what far-reaching effects your connections will have.

Meeting Manners Matter

- Be the first to arrive. You can pick up golden nuggets of intelligence in the "meeting before the meeting." The same goes for lingering at the end.

- Speak up so others can hear you.

- Sit up and don't fidget—slumping and fidgeting communicate boredom and negligence.

- Never attack someone directly. Whatever points you score are rarely worth acquiring an enemy. Even if someone's comment was ridiculous, preface your response with "I see where you're coming from, but . . ."

- Always sound nice—especially when what you're saying isn't.

"Soft Skills" Help You Keep the Job Once You Get It

I know from tough experience how large a role soft skills play in our career success. When I first started working as an investment analyst on Wall Street, I had a degree in English literature and lacked the same financial background as my colleagues. My first performance review was less than stellar, and it was clear I had to raise my game. Instead of racing to leave after a long day at the office, I began staying past midnight to pore over finance textbooks. More importantly, however, I put my soft skills to work overtime. On an early restructuring deal, the lawyer was a woman in her early forties. There were very few female role models on deal teams, and despite being twenty years her junior, I wasn't shy about initiating conversation with her and asking her to explain legal terms. She became a kind of mentor and invited me to the coveted Women in Restructuring luncheons that no one at my level attended.

I also worked on forging strong bonds with clients. As the most junior member on a debt restructuring deal team for a hotel casino, I joined in a lunch with a client in Kentucky. I was tempted (as a self-confessed carnivore) by the baby back ribs on the menu. After giving it some thought—we were in the South, and our client was a heavyset, jolly, middle-aged man wearing jeans—I decided that if there was ever an appropriate time to order baby back ribs in front of a client, it was now. I went for it, and of course dug in with my fingers. My former supervisor later wrote in a recommendation letter, "She ordered baby back ribs (a move I would generally say is fairly aggressive), but the client loved her for it. Despite male dominance in the hotel and hospitality industries, Sara was able to create meaningful and lasting relationships with clients."

Pay attention to context, and you can make bold moves with confidence. As a result, something as seemingly insignificant as what dish you order in a restaurant can pay huge dividends. Obviously, I had to work on getting my hard skills up to speed, but many people don't realize that the hard skills won't work without the soft ones!

Feng Shui Tip: Now That You've Landed the Job

Finding your desk's commanding kao shan position, at home or in the office, is vital to your career success. The ideal setup is that you should be able to see the door without being directly in line with it when sitting at your desk. This is the power position of any room, including meeting rooms. I also like to have a wall behind me, which is what we call a *kao shan*, meaning a "back support mountain." The worst position is to sit facing the wall, unable to see the door, with your back exposed. This makes you vulnerable to office politics and backstabbing. Having your back to the door can also lead to a lack of control, support, and creativity in your work. Directly facing a wall limits growth.

When I visited the home of my Netflix makeover student Christy Aldred, I was shocked at how poorly arranged her home office was. Her desk was against the wall under the staircase, and when she sat there, she had her back to the room (vulnerable) with the staircase right above her head (pressure). The desk, covered with clutter, was hardly a place to get her thoughts in order. No wonder she was anxious and had difficulty rebooting her career.

CLIMBING THE LADDER

Be a Matchmaker

Connecting people is my one superpower. If you want to be "well connected" then you need to learn the power of connecting people—and every one of us can hone this superpower. Within moments of meeting somebody, I can discern exactly what they need. And if you rack your brain, you can almost always think of someone who can help them get it. Nothing gives me a thrill like matchmaking a worthwhile person with a worthwhile opportunity—and I've made quite a few work and love matches. I learned from the best.

I grew up in Hong Kong surrounded by the original super-connectors, my mother and my Hong Kong "aunties"—close (but not blood-related) friends of parents notorious for probing the younger generation about their love lives and future plans. At any of my mother's social gatherings, I could hear my aunties keenly connecting the dots and offering up resources and information. They couldn't help themselves. For example, once I got accepted to Georgetown, they immediately busied themselves lining me up with older Hong Kong children who they knew were existing students to show me the ropes. In reverse fashion, my Hong Kong aunties later requested that I share with younger family friends the secrets of getting into Harvard Business School.

Do you remember British anthropologist Robin Dunbar from Part One, who claimed each of us has 150 meaningful contacts (these are the people you might invite to a large party)? Superconnectors like the aunties have up to 1,500 meaningful contacts. I've never counted mine, but the number seems about right. And while there are supposedly six degrees of separation between everyone on earth, for superconnectors in the digital age, it's more like three or four.

While the following "commandments" might not make you an actual superconnector, they will help you strengthen and multiply your mutually beneficial connections with others.

The Six Commandments of Superconnectors

1. **It's not about the numbers: it's about the quality of relationships.** One of the "Ten Commandments" of Goldman Sachs, drawn up by former cochair John Whitehead, is "The respect of one man is worth more than acquaintance with one hundred." I would sometimes attend conferences when I was studying in the US, and there was always that one kid going around asking everyone for their

business cards. I would wince in vicarious embarrassment for him. The true power of networking is not in collecting as many contacts as possible, but rather in making worthwhile connections. They might be relatively few, but they are the interesting people with whom you share mutual respect and who could come in handy someday. Bonus points if they are superconnectors!

2. **Keep up with your connections.** Schedule regular catch-ups with useful acquaintances, especially if they are in a different industry. Lunch twice a year is enough to keep up with new trends.

3. **Enjoy the present; look to the future.** Trust isn't forged overnight, and good relationships are not strictly transactional. Enlightened self-interest means that both parties benefit. Relationships might not yield "rewards" for years. In the meantime, the relationship itself is the reward.

4. **It is better to give.** A superconnector knows that it's better to give (first) than to receive (first). The law of reciprocity requires that if you give something to another person, they feel indebted to you. All the better if you're actually motivated by a spirit of generosity.

5. **Be generous.** The more you invite and include people, the more you will be included in return. Don't be afraid of introducing people to each other. Being their common link will make you even more of an insider.

6. **Don't be offended if people you introduce become better friends than they are with you.** A truly successful connection is "self-supporting." Remove yourself as the intermediary or you'll tire yourself with unnecessary administrative work. The point is that these

connections are mutually beneficial, and that includes you! Once you make the introduction, let people handle their own relationships. You don't always have to be in the loop.

Stop Networking and Create Your Own Network

Creating connections is joyful community building, which is *not* the same as networking. Networking is transactional. While it is often presented as a distasteful yet necessary chore, it's actually inefficient. Tapping into an existing "network" is like going on a mass-market dating site without using filters. Your chances of finding what you are looking for are about as great as winning the lottery. What I propose in place of networking is creating your own network. Interestingly, it's more likely to be your acquaintances than your friends who are going to be helpful when you need a job or have some other requirement, so it's useful to expand your reach.

Now, some people are averse to connecting others or bringing different groups of friends together—either because they are territorial over their connections, or because they think it is awkward to introduce people who don't already know each other. I think the opposite. When people come together because of you, you become a central core of the community you create. It strengthens their bond to you and elevates you.

An example: Having grown up in Hong Kong, I have always been very interested in traditional Chinese medicine. Since living in mainland China, I often read up on ancient herbal formulations and remedies. I was on a work call with a journalist and, out of courtesy as an opening question, asked what she was working on. She replied that she had just interviewed an acupuncturist on the benefits of acupuncture for fertility. This piqued my interest, so I responded, "I'm doing research for a project in Eastern wellness! Can you introduce me to him?" I visited him a few days later and invited him to give a talk to my etiquette students. During this talk, he mentioned he was looking to shoot a documentary on acupuncture, and one of my students who is a producer ended up funding and developing his show. That's how connecting works.

In a similar vein—the people we work with don't need to be *just* people we work with—my etiquette students are more than merely clients. As a teacher and friend, I try to provide solutions to their problems. One such student was worried about the direction of her daughter's career. Judy was applying to college for art, but didn't have a strong enough arts portfolio. "There's more to the art world than being an artist," I said. "Let's get her a summer internship with an art gallery to add to her experience." Then I called a friend of mine who ran a gallery and said, "Do you need free labor? I have a bright and hardworking young woman who can intern for free this summer." I told each what they wanted to hear and poof, it came together. At the end of summer, my gallerist friend was grateful to me for providing him with a capable intern, my etiquette student was grateful that I provided her daughter with good experience that padded her resume, and her daughter enjoyed the internship so much that she continued interning part-time into the school year. Plus she ended up getting into the college she wanted!

Barter Your Social Capital

Connecting people who can supply things of mutual value is like the barter system—of social capital. You might think, *That's easy for Sara Jane to say, but my social connections are suffering from chronic neglect.* Maybe it will help to hear how I started my own superconnected community from scratch during Shanghai's epic sixty-day COVID lockdown in 2022.

Shortly after moving into my apartment, I left the country to shoot my Netflix show, so I barely knew my neighbors. Upon my return, the one-hundred-unit building had become a totally closed community overnight. No one was permitted to leave under any circumstances, even to buy groceries.

A few days into the lockdown, an elderly couple living two floors below me, whom I felt an instant kinship with since they were also from Hong Kong (we could speak Cantonese together), asked me if I had any flour or bananas. I didn't. The same day, however, I was lounging on my balcony, chatting with a couple on the balcony directly above. I offhandedly asked them if they had any flour, and when they said yes, I asked if they could give it to Shanley in Apartment 10D. Without delay, one of them took the stairs and dropped it off outside his door. The next day, a neighbor in our resident group chat whom I didn't know personally wrote, "I have extra bananas. Does anybody need some?" I immediately replied, "Apartment 10D needs bananas!" She ran over and deposited them outside Shanley's door. I had spontaneously morphed into an unofficial "ingredients" agent.

The following week, Shanley (obviously a big baker) needed eggs. I had some to spare, so I walked down two floors and left them outside his door. By the time I got upstairs, he had sent me a text message: "No need to run away. Two weeks have gone by and nobody in the compound has tested positive. Why don't you come back and have a glass of wine with me and Rebecca?" When I went downstairs to hang out with them, they offered me some delicious banana bread along with the wine. I suggested getting together with a few of the other neighbors to do a potluck. "How about the kind couple who gave you flour? And Jamie, the lady who gave you bananas?" Thus, a regular potluck dinner crew was formed, meeting three times a week and rotating homes. That is how we happily survived the remaining weeks of what would otherwise have been a depressing and lonely lockdown. What's more, we became a support group, sharing information, jokes, and recipes. Shanley and Rebecca became my adoptive godparents in the building, caring for me like a daughter and spoiling me with treats.

The "ingredients" network eventually spread to encompass the whole building. Enwei, the man who originally supplied Shanley with flour, was a hotel manager. Since we could not leave the building to shop for food (not that any stores were open), he and his partner, Andreas, took on the incredibly complicated and thankless task of coordinating group food orders for the entire building. This helped to spark what became the generous, friendly, and caring culture of our community. In fact, our compound went viral on social media for our positivity. In a big city like Shanghai where it's easy to feel alone as we fend for ourselves, the sixty-day lockdown brought out the best in humanity—sharing and caring.

Fake It Till You Make It

"Important people like to deal with other important people" is another of the original Ten Commandments from John Whitehead at Goldman Sachs. When you know what people want and have the power to ensure they get it, you become important, no matter what size pond you swim in. My first few years in China I hosted a monthly dinner in conjunction with Temple Restaurant Beijing. The intimate table consisted of twelve guests who each bought an expensive "ticket" for a formal meal whose proceeds were donated to a local charity. So every month, I was hustling to sell tickets to interesting guests to create just the right mix for a special evening.

My preference was to have representatives of various industries, a foreign diplomat, one of my etiquette students, and potential corporate clients—plus an even male-to-female ratio. It was certainly a brain teaser! For one such dinner, I invited the ambassador of Botswana. I had met him not long before at an event, so I sent him a message and informed him of three other guests who would be attending, along with brief background information about each one. I knew that his work in China meant promoting Botswana and finding investment, so two of the guests I mentioned were in tourism media, and the third was one of the most prominent trade and investment lawyers in Beijing. The ambassador accepted on the spot, which only made me think more highly of him.

I confess I used a bit of chutzpah here when I said the lawyer was attending since he hadn't yet RSVP'd. The most famous Hollywood agent of all time, Irving "Swifty" Lazar, often used this technique to sell books and other properties he hadn't been retained to represent. For example, he would tell Madonna, say, that Simon & Schuster was interested in doing a book with her, and then he would go to the publishing company and announce that Madonna was interested in doing a book. And voilà! He once said in an interview, "The greatest fun is to sell something you don't represent at all. If I like something I go out and sell it. I usually manage to get paid anyway." So when the lawyer replied an hour later saying he was leaving for a business trip that day and wouldn't be able to attend, I didn't panic. Instead, after a moment's thought, I wrote back, "That's too bad. The ambassador of Botswana is coming and I was planning on seating you next to him. Let me know if your schedule changes!" A few hours later, he told me he changed his flight to leave the next day so he could come to my dinner.

> **Pro Tip:** When you understand how to bring value to people, you become important, and important people want to know you.

The Old Boys/Girls Network

The system of personal connections, social networks, and influential alliances used to open doors for business and facilitate deals in China is called *guanxi* (pronounced "gwan shee"). Guanxi is based on personal trust and strong relationships, and it often involves moral obligations and exchanging favors. Although the idea of reciprocal obligation as a way of doing business exists in all cultures, the masters of guanxi tend to be Asian and Arab. Because the legal systems in these cultures are relatively underdeveloped and weakly enforced, relationships are typically valued more than laws. Therefore, powerful guanxi, based on the strength of your network, is synonymous with being well-connected and able to make things happen.

Guanxi is relationship-building, and no matter what culture you inhabit, it can help you in your career. A savvy European friend of mine demonstrated his understanding of guanxi when he parachuted into China to manage a large corporation. He didn't speak Mandarin, let alone have any useful connections. But he immediately hired someone with a strong background in government relations who came recommended by a friend. Within months, he was able to take meetings with very high level people, and during the height of COVID restrictions received the impossible perk of doing an inbound fourteen-day quarantine at his home, bypassing the law of doing it in a centralized quarantine hotel.

This goes to show that even if you don't have the relationships yourself, you can quickly integrate by hiring or aligning yourself with somebody who does. Form one solid relationship with a core superconnector, and tap into their guanxi to make it work for you.

The best example of guanxi in the US and UK is what is known as the "old boy network," where strings are pulled and things get done behind the scenes based on trust and the tacit expectation of repayment in return. The problem is that this network is based as much on exclusion as inclusion. It is still going strong in the world of finance, as I saw when I worked as an investment banking analyst on Wall Street in my first two years out of college. I was never invited to male colleagues' fly-fishing trips or evenings at cigar bars. I most definitely missed out on a huge chunk of guanxi building. We did women's lunches . . . but it wasn't quite the same when the heavy hitters and decision-makers at the firm were all men.

Another downside of guanxi (no matter where it is found) is that it is often associated with corruption and can lead to dangerous reciprocal obligations, insider trading, and nepotism. Many firms would rather hire somebody they have guanxi with than the most qualified person available. It is more often used to keep people out than to welcome them in.

Despite obstacles and possible pitfalls, the principle holds that relationship-building is useful in your career. If you spend time building your own network and tapping into a preexisting powerful network of those inclined to help you, it will be there when you need to call upon it in the future.

Pay It Forward

After I graduated from Harvard Business School, my classmate Krizia reached out to me three times in a row to introduce me to new business opportunities, never asking me for help or introductions in return. A relative of mine happened to be friends with her, and when they saw each other at dinner, he thanked her for sending opportunities my way. "I like to pay it forward," she said, smiling. When Krizia started her own company a few years later, all the introductions and generosity she had bestowed upon others were returned to her. Everyone who knew her went out of their way to help, myself included, and she received everything she needed.

Wharton management professor Adam Grant, researching how people differ in their approach to reciprocity, divided them into three types: givers, takers, and matchers (those who believe in tit for tat). Krizia is a great example of a "giver," someone who doesn't think about the short-term benefits when doing something to help others. As her story shows, when you pay it forward, you will be paid back many times over.

So, focus on cultivating goodwill, not the quick payoff. I routinely treat my corporate clients to lunch. Once, I reached out to a luxury watch brand with which I had collaborated by providing etiquette workshops to its customers. When I invited the marketing executive to a meal, she messaged back, "I've just left the company, so you probably want to invite someone else who is still there." I paused for a second before replying, "Then you have no excuse to say you're too busy to have lunch with me!" She was pleasantly surprised. Even if you are networking, don't make it seem like networking. During lunch, I asked her if she could introduce me to other luxury watch brands. Right afterward, she introduced me to two that I pitched for business and won!

PROTECTING YOUR TIME
AND PEACE OF MIND

Don't Squander Your Time and Talents

There are limits to the free expenditure of energy I've been advocating. My natural tendency is to be generous and helpful, but recently I've begun to stop squandering what are, unfortunately, limited resources. Recently, my close friend Alice asked me to speak with a friend of hers about applying to HBS. She confessed that she had asked our mutual friend Krizia first but that Krizia had turned her down. After looking at the woman's resume, Krizia had said she wasn't HBS material. I agreed to look at the resume since she was Alice's friend. Even though she was completely unqualified, and it was one of the worst I had ever seen from an MBA candidate, I agreed to speak with her due to my friendship with Alice. What a waste of twenty minutes! The woman asked me questions with answers that could readily be found on the school's website. Her vague and meandering conversation made it clear she wasn't going to get into any business school, if she even bothered applying.

> Even the Bible says, "Don't cast your pearls before swine." In other words, save your generosity for those who can benefit from it.

I didn't feel great about the encounter, but I couldn't blame Alice. I'm responsible for my own time, and I should have taken a page from Krizia's book and said no right away. Krizia is known as being bubbly and generous, which she is, but she's also smart about setting limits. I felt more respect for her rather than less when I discovered what she'd done—and vowed to emulate her behavior in the future. What Krizia was so good at was setting boundaries.

How to Say No

Knowing how to draw a boundary in a firm yet elegant way will improve your life immeasurably at work and in every other area. This first occurred to me when my colleague Lindsay held a morning meeting that ran well into the afternoon although we were supposed to get lunch together that day. When the meeting finally ended, she stormed into my office, complaining, "Gosh, that woman would not stop talking! She went on for three hours. I can't believe I had to endure that. She simply did not want to leave!"

Hungry and irritated, I said, "Why are you victimizing yourself and making it sound like you had no choice? You are in control of your own time and how long someone spends with you. Especially when you are the chair of your meeting. All you needed to do was look at your watch and say, 'Well! I am so glad you took the time to come by today. I'm afraid I need to head out for my lunch appointment now.'" Lindsay didn't want to be rude, but she gained nothing by failing to establish a boundary except a feeling of resentment.

In other cases, we need to politely decline unreasonable requests from a supervisor. If you report directly to the person making the request (i.e., you are their trusted "right hand"), you might have the standing to respectfully disagree. Make sure you give the matter serious consideration before you approach them. If it's a capacity issue, say, "This sounds like an exciting opportunity, but I have my hands full with XYZ this week. How can I rearrange my task list to accommodate your request?" Basically you're telling them, "If you want me to do this, you can't have both." Let them choose for you. You're not saying no, you're just saying it's not humanly possible and forcing them to make a managerial choice.

If you straight up disagree, suggest another idea. It's possible your supervisor will hear you out and you can propose a better solution. If all else fails, you can decline and make it look like a joke, as long as you're not sarcastic. But in any case, when you say no, prepare yourself for your boss to be peeved. Don't delay out of fear and wait too long to decline. Give your supervisor the opportunity to reassign the project to someone else.

If you're not the right hand, think about where you are in the hierarchy. If you are several rungs down, appeal to a trusted person in between you and the senior member to intercede for you. This is particularly useful if someone from another department (not your boss) asks you to do something.

Surviving Micromanagers

There's nothing worse than having a micromanaging boss (make sure you don't become one yourself). First of all, look within. Do you require micromanaging? If the answer is no, learn to push back. Ask for room to work more independently by saying, "Can I run with this on my own and check back with you at the first milestone?" Showing your supervisor that they will still be involved can help make them feel more comfortable backing off.

As a means of last resort, flash a huge smile—with teeth— and say, "Don't you trust me? I'm sure you've got better things to do with your time than to inject yourself into the details of this project!"

Etiquette Is Armor

Closely allied with drawing boundaries in a graceful and appropriate way is putting up with other people's bad manners, and nowhere is this more true than at work. One story of Queen Elizabeth II at work encapsulates this truth so well that it's practically a parable.

In 1961, the queen welcomed Yuri Gagarin, the first man in space, to Buckingham Palace for a reception followed by breakfast. As they were sipping their coffee before the meal, Gagarin reached under the table and stroked the queen's leg just above the knee. She somehow managed to keep a smile on her face, and he later explained that he had done so because he wanted to make sure she was actually human. The queen's self-restraint was admirable, but what was truly impressive was that she didn't take the opportunity for rudeness that was served to her on a silver platter alongside breakfast. When Gagarin confessed to her that he had no idea how to use all the silverware, she responded kindly, saying, "My dear Mr. Gagarin, I was brought up in this palace—but believe me, I still don't know in which order I should use all these forks and knives."

Rudeness responded to with rudeness begets more rudeness. Just look at Twitter! Etiquette is about making the world more, rather than less, civilized. Maintaining your composure when others are slinging mud keeps your hands (and conscience) clean.

I stumbled on the power of etiquette as armor when I was seventeen years old and my parents set me up with a summer internship at an electronics company in Beijing. The company culture was stereotypically Chinese, and coming from a prep school in New England, I was out of my comfort zone but thoroughly enjoyed the adventure. Halfway through the summer, we had a marketing department team building outing at a karaoke bar—drinking, singing, and playing dice. Our department boss got extremely drunk and tried to make a pass at me in full view of all of our colleagues. I artfully dodged him without a fuss, wearing an unperturbed smile and clueless look. For the rest of the evening, I moved around the karaoke table flanked at all times by friendly colleagues, careful to ensure that I was always at the farthest possible point from him. Otherwise, I acted perfectly normal. He ended up getting so drunk that he smashed a glass on the floor and made a scene, after which two colleagues took him home.

The next morning, there was a hush on our floor as the department boss arrived noticeably late. Once he sat down behind his desk, he called out my name. Everyone watched me walk into his office. Even though I felt embarrassed and awkward, nothing in my behavior or speech gave it away. I had the same spring in my step as I always did, and looked him in the eye and smiled as usual, saying, "Good morning, boss!" He gave me a sheepish look, lowered his voice, and said, "I'm sorry about last night . . ." So many thoughts raced through my head: this was my parents' friend's company and things could get complicated. I definitely did not want to make a scene, and I wanted to squelch any rumors of him liking me. What was the best reaction?

I jumped in and countered brightly, "I don't know what you're talking about! Thank you for taking us out, boss! Would you like some tea? We just boiled some water in the kitchen!" and then I went about my day as I always did. The incident became a nonissue.

This was China twenty years ago. I might behave differently now, in light of the #MeToo movement. I hope at the very least that I would have felt empowered to leave the karaoke bar as soon as he'd made me feel uncomfortable! As it was, in the absence of other supports, I let etiquette be my armor and completed my internship with flying colors.

Rehearse Your Response

Etiquette can help you maintain distance between yourself and another person in a way that will not offend. Maintain a mental checklist for polite behavior toward someone you don't like or to show that their behavior doesn't affect you (even if you were provoked). Pleasantly asking the standard questions such as "How are you? What have you been up to these days?" or "Can you believe this weather we're having?" will instantly neutralize the encounter.

I continue to use this tool on a regular basis. Soon after I started my finishing school, my business partner, Rebecca, put a meeting on my calendar with a woman who she said wanted to meet me. I was overwhelmed and exhausted since we had just opened our doors, but Rebecca said this middle-aged Singaporean lady was a fellow alumna of the Swiss finishing school we had attended and very persistent. I welcomed her warmly and invited her to sit down on an elegant sofa. Before I could even say anything, she smacked her lips and said, "Har-vard. Business. School. Harvard. Business. School." I was gob-smacked, because she kept on repeating it without any context. I smiled at her searchingly and said, "Yes, that's right, that's where I went for my MBA." Then she said, "Harvard Business School is known for turning out the worst leaders in society because they have no feelings for other people." I was shocked that those were the first words out of her mouth. As a fellow graduate of our fin-ishing school, why was she so rude? Did *she* have any feelings for other people? I was inwardly furious but merely chuckled and said, "Well, every school churns out a few bad eggs. But I'm not sure we can apply that to the whole school body." The next sentence out of her mouth was yet another insult. I entertained her for five min-utes, and then smiled sweetly and said, "Oh! I see our colleague motioning me to receive an important call. Unfortunately, I have to leave now, but Rebecca will be more than happy to take care of you." Etiquette was the armor I used to extract myself from the terrible lady from Singapore while maintaining my composure.

> "Truly powerful people don't explain why they want respect. They simply don't engage someone who doesn't give it to them."
>
> —SHERRY ARGOV

Like Water off a Duck's Back

When people are negative, they're saying more about themselves than about you. One of my favorite examples occurred in response to a January 2023 *New York Times* Style profile of me. For the cover image, the photographer had creatively asked me to spear a cupcake with my knife. It was so original and unexpected that I reveled in it, but a male etiquette instructor from the UK commented on Instagram, "I mean Ms. Ho isn't holding the fork correctly and you wouldn't use a knife on a cupcake at all, yet alone spear it." A friend read this aloud to me on the phone, and we had a good giggle. Rather than feeling offended, I thought it was funny that he took his own profession so seriously that he couldn't see that the photo was meant in jest. Remember, when you point a finger, three fingers point back at you!

Don't feed the negative, and it will fade away from neglect. Instead, use the law of attraction to focus on and multiply the positive. We can't control others; we can only control ourselves.

> "Success seems to be connected with action. Successful people keep moving. They make mistakes, but they don't quit."
>
> —CONRAD HILTON

According to Carl Jung, one of the brilliant pioneers of modern psychology, "What you resist not only persists, but will grow in size." That's why it's important to ignore negative feedback when it's not constructive. Don't give energy to it.

If You Don't Know How to React, Smile

A powerful way to neutralize negativity is to smile. Believe me, this is more Machiavelli than Pollyanna: one of my secrets—especially in the workplace—is to use a smile as a tool for when I don't know how to react. Think of the last time someone challenged you or asked you a difficult or impossible question. You don't always have to provide a verbal response or defense. Sometimes our minds simply don't work that quickly. If someone is looking at you expectantly for a response and you are at a loss for words, shocked, confused, embarrassed, or merely shy—just smile. A smile is ambiguous and open to interpretation. At the very least, it will buy you time.

> "A smile is the chosen vehicle of all ambiguities."
> —HERMAN MELVILLE

I use this tactic in China when I don't understand an ancient proverb, when I am in London and puzzled by bone-dry humor, or when I am in New York and don't understand the latest slang. A smile makes me look mysterious, satisfied, clever, or connected, as needed. It is the Swiss Army knife of responses—an all-purpose tool.

But smiling does not come naturally to everyone. As a little girl, I had a habit of frowning. My parents thought it was due to poor eyesight and took me to get my vision checked—my vision was fine. As an adult, my resting face is not a smiling face, and when I don't wear an expression I look very serious. Over the years, people I have met for the first time have sometimes said, "Before I met you, I thought you looked very unapproachable. But in real life you are so nice and down-to-earth!"

For an etiquette expert, looking serious and scary doesn't add points. It's something I've come to be mindful of—especially when on camera or doing a photo shoot. My colleague Rebecca would always stand behind the production crew to remind me if I went back into resting bitch face. To get my attention, she'd waggle her hands next to her face and flash an exaggerated grin.

My mother used to say there are three types of people in this world. One type learns from their own mistakes. The second type learns from other people's mistakes. The third type never learns . . . If you can't be in the first category, try not to fall into the third!

The benefits of smiling, even aside from its utility, are numerous. Studies have found that people who smile are perceived to be more attractive, which is powerful motivation in itself, but smiling doesn't send signals only outward to others but also inward to ourselves. Thich Nhat Hanh said, "Sometimes your joy is the source of your smile, but sometimes your smile can be the source of your joy." I don't think he was talking about the facial feedback hypothesis, but he could have been. This widely accepted hypothesis states that a facial expression like smiling or frowning provides feedback to the brain that reinforces, or even creates, an emotional experience.

Smiling prompts the body to release endorphins along with the happiness neurotransmitter dopamine and stress-reducing serotonin. That may be why smiling lowers blood pressure and heart rate in tense situations, builds immunity, and even contributes to longevity—a pretty painless way to improve your health. And a smile is so contagious that you can even catch one from yourself. Next time you pass a mirror, smile at yourself for fifteen seconds. It's a proven way to make yourself feel happier (just make sure no one else is around).

When Someone Criticizes You, Thank Them

Welcoming constructive criticism is the most powerful tool there is for career success, at least I have found it so. We've all seen what happens to leaders when they surround themselves with "yes people," and if your only feedback comes from family and friends who agree with whatever you say, you might never get an honest appraisal of your actual performance or learn how you can improve. So, as painful as it is, you should be grateful for feedback that lets you know when you have fallen short. I'll share some tips on how to deal with constructive criticism, but first, here's a recent experience in which I needed to be reminded to practice the etiquette I preach.

One of the early press invitations I received after the airing of *Mind Your Manners* was from a television show. The segment— taped in the US—was so much fun, the audience roared with laughter, and the host was very friendly toward me. It went very well. Or so I thought.

I have a close relationship with Donovan, one of the executive producers of *Mind Your Manners*. He is a westernized Singaporean who pushes me to deliver 200 percent on set but is also someone with whom I can kick back and have a beer. A month after I appeared on the show, at the end of a work-related video call, Donovan said, "By the way, I'm telling you this because I can be totally transparent with you, and because you know I have your best interests at heart. I got a call today from a friend in the industry, and she said that the feedback from the television set was that you were telling people what to do, and that you must have felt like you were really famous from the success of *Mind Your Manners*."

"A man must be big enough to admit his mistakes, smart enough to profit from them, and strong enough to correct them."

—JOHN C. MAXWELL

My jaw dropped. Because I have never thought I was ever too famous or too good for anything or anyone. My Tiger Mother made sure of that!

Donovan continued, "I told her that that is absolutely not what you are like, and that if I told you, you would be horrified to have come across that way. But remember what I told you in the past, about how Americans are softer and more 'feel good' than Asians in their communication style, and how Asian bluntness can come across as too direct?"

I did remember, and the first thing I said, when it sank in, was, "Wow, thank you for telling me." Then I added, "I feel so terrible that someone on set felt that way. Please thank Julie for telling you to tell me. I'm really glad you gave me this feedback."

He laughed. "I know you and I knew you would take this well, as you have done with all my previous feedback over the years. Just take some time to absorb it, and be more mindful, especially when you are in the States."

After the call, I immediately raced back in my mind to whom I could have offended on set. I had spoken with the script writer ahead of the show, and she subsequently emailed the Netflix team, "It was great speaking with Sara. She's so lovely!!" Then could it have been my minder? But in general I am punctual and eager to be where they want me at any time. Aha! It must have been the makeup artist. That was the only tense encounter I'd had on set.

I have a very definite idea of how I want my makeup done, as Asian faces are less contoured than Caucasian faces. I had explained this to her and offered that I would apply the blush and eyeshadow myself. "I know how to apply blush," she snapped back. After I conveyed that my single eyelid doesn't take red-toned eyeshadow well— because it makes me look puffy—she put a red-toned eyeshadow on my eyelids and said, "It looks red now, but it won't on camera." I wanted to push back but was intimidated and afraid of upsetting her further. When I left her chair, I felt confused and conflicted, but didn't want to give energy to the encounter and soon forgot it.

I later got confirmation that it was indeed the makeup artist. As I replayed the encounter in my mind, I reflected inward. For high-achieving Asians like me, the stereotype is to be blunt and straightforward. I am direct, my mother was direct, and most of my Chinese friends are . . . direct. Having spent the last decade living in China, sometimes my communication style tends toward bullet points. It comes across in my show—I'm not Mother Teresa. I'm Miss Manners with a touch of Machiavelli. However, that is no excuse for making others feel "less than." So, I was very grateful to receive this bit of feedback, which served as a check to rein me in and remind me that not everyone I interact with is accustomed to my style.

Six Tips for Processing Constructive Criticism

1. Keep an open mind. As hard as it is, try not to get defensive or upset when you receive constructive criticism. Instead, try

to listen to what the other person is saying and consider their perspective.

2. Remember that the criticism is of your behavior, not of your entire being. This will help you preserve your self-confidence as you absorb what is difficult to hear.

3. Look for the value in the criticism. Constructive criticism is meant to help you improve, so try to identify what you can learn or take away from the feedback.

4. Don't take it personally. It can be easy to feel attacked or get upset when you receive criticism, but try to remember that the other person is offering their perspective in order to help you grow.

5. Be grateful. Even if it's hard to hear, be thankful for the other person's willingness to take the risk of sharing their perspective to help you improve.

6. Use the criticism as a chance to reflect on your own actions and consider ways you can improve in the future. It's not about being perfect—it's about becoming a better version of yourself.

Forget What Hurt You, but Don't Forget What It Taught You

There is a Chinese proverb that says, "Defeat isn't bitter if you don't swallow it."

Once you've extracted the kernel of truth from an experience, don't let what others do or say ruin your day, and don't let their negativity extend into your thoughts. To be wronged is nothing unless you continue to remember it.

Master the Art of the Apology

Sometimes, the criticism we receive makes it clear that we owe an apology. In any relationship—whether with a boss, coworker, employee, client, romantic partner, family member, friend, or even stranger—we may make a mistake. Doing something wrong may not have been our choice. But righting a wrong certainly is. The way to apologize properly, if the offense is serious, is to do it as soon as possible. The longer you wait, the greater the temptation to cover it up, the harder it is to apologize, and the more persuasive the apology will need to be. As La Rochefoucauld said, "Most of our faults are more pardonable than the means we use to conceal them." We've all had the experience of digging ourselves in deeper as we try to hide some misdeed.

"A stiff apology is a second insult . . . The injured party does not want to be compensated because he has been wronged; he wants to be healed because he has been hurt."

—G. K. CHESTERTON

Explain why you did what you did, but acknowledge that it is no excuse, that you feel bad about it, and that it won't happen again. One particularly maddening line to avoid is "I'm sorry you feel that way," which suggests that the fault lies with the other person's reaction rather than your behavior. When someone has been wronged, they want to know you are truly sorry. They need you to understand and own what you did and how you made them feel. Don't be defensive. Never say, "I did this, but you did that." Even if what happened was not 100 percent your fault, the apology concerns only your part in it. Instead of justifying your behavior, say, "I'm sorry for doing that. And this is an important lesson for me, so I'll be more aware next time." If you have a personal relationship, validate their feelings by telling them, "I hear you and if I were you, I would be upset too." Apologies should come from the heart, or at least seem that way.

Beware of Envy, the Green Monster

"Of the seven deadly sins, only envy is no fun at all," Joseph Epstein quips in deadly seriousness. Overeating (gluttony), procrastinating (sloth), feeling superior (pride), righteous indignation (anger), sleeping around (lust), and good old-fashioned greed all have their charms and are delicious in small doses. But envy? Whether feeling it or inciting it, it can destroy you. Envy is pure pain, and impossible to eradicate once it infects you or others. It is everyone's dirty little secret, giving rise to more bad behavior than all the other deadly sins combined. We'll do anything not to admit feeling it—even to ourselves.

> "If you want enemies, excel your friends; but if you want friends, let your friends excel you."
>
> —FRANÇOIS DE LA ROCHEFOUCAULD

Envy eats away at you from the inside out. The only defense against it is to prevent it from taking root in the first place. When I meet successful women, I immediately see myself as a student and try to learn from them. To be in awe is a protection against envy. It is harder when the person is a peer; in that case, try to be generous and genuinely happy for those who have what you want, always remembering not to compare other people's outsides with your own insides. You never really know what is going on in another person's life.

As for inciting envy, social media seems designed to trumpet one's good fortune, but many Middle Eastern traditions encourage possessors of wealth, happiness, and beauty to hide them from those who would wish us ill. This sentiment is captured in a line written by Lebanese poet Kahlil Gibran: "Travel and tell no one, live a true love story and tell no one, live happily and tell no one, people ruin beautiful things." So how do we protect ourselves from the metaphorical "evil eye" in a world where everyone seems to know everything? One way is to use self-deprecating humor to neutralize envy. Another is to avail ourselves of the pratfall effect, which is a tendency for those who are considered highly competent to be perceived as more likable when they commit an everyday gaffe than those who don't. A classic example is Jennifer Lawrence tripping on her way up the red carpet to receive an Oscar. This only works if you're trying to neutralize envy, not if you're already perceived as mediocre, so don't go blundering in an effort to be likable unless you have a specific goal.

Usually, though, modesty and a bit of self-deprecation work wonders to nip envy in the bud. I attended a Harvard Business School alumni social where someone's husband commented to his wife (who was a few years younger than I) that she had to "catch up" with my entrepreneurship path. I immediately went into neutralization overdrive. I am extra careful not to incite envy in wives or girlfriends, especially when I like the couple and want to see them again. I said, "Heavens, definitely do not follow my example. To this day, my business school friends tease me for having the most unscalable business model! I mean, how do

I scale a high-end finishing school when the students only want me to teach?" By exposing my own business weakness, I made haste to short-circuit any possible envious feelings.

The problem with envy at work, aside from how awful it feels, is that it is counterproductive. When you envy others, you're unable to build a network in which their advancement is yours as well. As John F. Kennedy famously said, "A rising tide raises all boats." Remember that if you're ever tempted to undermine a colleague. Success is not a zero-sum game, and when we approach it with an abundance mentality in which there is enough to go around for everyone, we are more likely to succeed ourselves.

Work Hard and Play Hard

In the article for the *New York Times* Style section, I was quoted as saying I believe in "working hard and playing hard." The interviewer later told me her editors were fascinated by my party girl side, and in fact it was the first time I had revealed it in an interview. I told her that at Harvard Business School I spent most of my time "partying until dawn," and that when I worked on Wall Street fresh out of college, the harder I worked the more I wanted to go clubbing. Even when I first started my finishing school in China, my business partner, Rebecca, would give me long lists of what NOT to do and what NOT to say. She knew me too well. But it was never a conflict for me—I never felt that being an etiquette teacher should restrain me from getting drunk or going dancing. In fact, as a Sagittarius, having fun and going dancing are part of my DNA.

I always say there's a time and place for everything. As I told my student Stephanie Osifo in the first episode of *Mind Your Manners*, I had no objection to her white fishnet minidress as long as she wore it only to the club. That's a good example of the issue of context. Context is key, as always. But social media has introduced a wrinkle, which is that the context in which you do something is often not the context in which it will be shared with the world. Especially in a work context, you should be extra cautious about who sees you doing what, in real life or on social media. Many people have lost (or failed to get) jobs because of ill-advised (or mean-spirited) postings that came back to haunt them. Beware of envy—someone might be waiting for the opportunity to bring you down a peg. Don't do or say anything in public that you'd be mortified to share or have shared by someone else (which is another way of saying, be discreet).

> Before making a big decision, I always apply the Rule of 5. What will the repercussions of my actions be in 5 *minutes,* 5 *days,* and 5 *years?*

TECHNIQUES FROM MISS MACHIAVELLI

Weaponize Silence

Americans love the energy of bouncing ideas off of one another. In New York, where I used to live, people talk over each other all the time. The French, too, are notorious interrupters. In other countries, interrupting may be inappropriate, but in France it is simply a way to express your interest in the other person and the conversation. This behavior is typical of what's known as "talking cultures."

By contrast, Asian and many Nordic countries are "listening cultures," where silence can be more eloquent than words. The Chinese pause before answering to show respect and to indicate that they have given your statement due consideration. Of course this behavior is not restricted to specific cultures. When I was an analyst on Wall Street, we were trained to mute ourselves on conference calls unless we were speaking, and to this day my finger is always hovering over the mute button. I find that it keeps me from interrupting, and people are often pleasantly surprised by it. Silence can also be used in other ways: to save face or to intimidate. Nothing conveys authority as effectively as silence. On the other hand, we might simply be suggesting that we are relaxed enough in someone's company to enjoy a quiet moment. It is easy to see how these cross-cultural differences could lead to conflicting interpretations.

In America, as in many other Western cultures, silence is often viewed as awkward or uncomfortable. It is seen to indicate lack of connection or understanding between the people speaking. As a result, people in Western cultures may feel pressure to fill silences with conversation, even if they have nothing particular to say. From personal experience, I have discovered that the more nervous someone is, the less silence they can tolerate. In fact, studies have shown that Americans are unable to tolerate a silence of longer than about *one second* before they chomp at the bit to fill up space. In China, by contrast, silence is viewed as a natural and important part of conversation. It is not necessarily regarded as a sign of discomfort or a lack of something to say, but rather as a way to allow space for reflection or contemplation. It can also be used to show respect or deference to the person speaking or to the conversation itself. So, pay attention to where you are and who's around. Like everything else, silence depends on context.

In negotiations and other adversarial conversations, silence can be the most powerful weapon there is. The great biographer Robert Caro claimed it was always the awkward silences in interviews that yielded the greatest revelations. When you ask a question and someone responds, wait an extra two or three seconds after they finish their sentence before you reply. They will probably fill the silence with more than they originally meant to say. Similarly, the first law of business negotiation is that she who speaks first loses. Pretending to care less than your opponent puts you in a position of power, and you can never learn anything while you're talking.

It's also a smart idea to get comfortable with silence in social situations. If you can train yourself not to jump in after that one second (it can be hard, but keep at it!), you'll find that people often volunteer intimate information about themselves or take the conversation in an unexpected direction. Alternatively, you might find that there's a delightful intimacy in that shared moment of nonverbal communication. There are as many varieties of silence as of speech—don't ruin a good silence. The fact is that conversation is a combination of speaking and silence. We need training to keep silent, but unless we're painfully shy, most of us don't need encouragement to talk.

The 20-Second Rule

I always advise using the 20-second rule to monitor yourself. Don't speak for more than 20 seconds at a time. Think of conversation as a traffic signal. In the first 20 seconds you have a green light—the person you're chatting with is engaged and enjoying the conversation. But if you go beyond 20 seconds, you've hit a yellow light. Caution! You're edging toward boring. At the 40-second mark, you're officially self-obsessed. Red light!

Make Someone Invest in You (Ben Franklin's Maxim)

In his memoir, Benjamin Franklin describes an "old maxim" that helped him along in his political career: "He that has once done you a kindness will be more ready to do you another, than he whom you yourself have obliged." It's counterintuitive, but someone is more likely to think well of you if *they* have done *you* a favor than if you have done one for them. As Dale Carnegie put it in *How to Win Friends and Influence People*, asking someone for a favor is a "subtle but effective form of flattery." It implies that they have something you need.

I have found that this principle, also known as the Ben Franklin effect, works even on insignificant things. For example, I'll stop someone in the hall and ask to quickly pick their brain on a matter or ask them to recommend a restaurant for a client lunch. It's not that I really need the help most of the time, but these small interactions create a bond that can be built upon.

Use Humor to Disarm

Perhaps you have heard the phrase "grace under pressure," and it is a commendable quality to strive for. But how can you find such grace in dark moments if you're not superhuman? My answer is simple: humor. As Oscar Wilde said, "Life is too important to be taken seriously," especially in times of difficulty.

As a tool for success in the workplace, humor is both powerful and often overlooked. As the findings of an eight-experiment study published in 2017 have shown, a well-timed joke at work can make you appear more confident and competent, and even increase your chances of being considered for a leadership role. Humor can help you dodge uncomfortable questions, as—famously—when Ronald Reagan was questioned during the second presidential debate about whether his age would affect his ability to serve a second term. (At seventy-three, Reagan was the oldest president in American history and had appeared tired during the first debate.) Reagan responded, "I will not make age an issue of this campaign. I am not going to exploit, for political purposes, my opponent's youth and inexperience." The audience, including his opponent, Walter Mondale, burst out laughing. Mondale later said that this was the moment he realized he would lose the election.

I recognize that because I'm an etiquette expert, people are naturally a bit nervous around me, especially my students. Many don't know that I am in fact a real prankster and love telling a dirty joke, but this trait is on full display in my Netflix show. In the final episode, "But It's a Tail Dude," I introduced Chinese immigrant Bunny Yan to feng shui. It was her first experience, and she knew little about it. I entered her home with the feng shui master along with the camera crew. Understandably, she was a bit nervous regarding what he would reveal about her *on camera*. So I put her at ease with some humor by explaining, "Master Philip is working away doing really precise measurements, and based on that will determine your ideal wealth position, health position, marriage position, and sexual position," which led her to giggle, and immediately eliminated all of her nervousness. As a famous late-night comedian observed, "You cannot laugh and be afraid at the same time."

Humor can also communicate tricky messages that can't be addressed head-on. My favorite example was when Madeleine Albright, then secretary of state, wore an enormous bug brooch at her first meeting with the Russian foreign minister—after discovering that the Soviets had bugged the State Department. Cheeky but powerful.

Of course, humor—like everything else—depends on context. One reason that humor increases people's estimation of your confidence is that it's inherently risky. If a joke goes wrong, it can go very wrong. So, when in doubt—don't.

Use the Law of the Last Look

People always talk about first impressions, but equally important and too often neglected is the Law of the Last Look. Not to be confused with the legal term of a similar name, the Law of the Last Look depends on the "recency effect," our tendency to remember recent events more clearly than previous ones. Even if the earlier events are more numerous or significant, we overvalue the thing that just happened. That's why in a jury trial the defense, which presents its argument last, has the advantage. First impressions, too, have disproportionate weight. It's the stuff in the middle that we forget.

This principle has many applications: the last thing you say in an interview, the last entry in a text or email exchange, whether you followed through on something you promised, the last time you reached out to someone . . .

When you maintain your network, for example, you stay top of mind. On a trip to London recently, I bumped into a realtor who had helped me sell a house. I hadn't seen Sam in years, and we were in a random little café, but we exchanged a few pleasantries. When I got home, I found an email from him with his new contact information and a link to some of the properties he was representing. A month later, when I was catching up with a friend, she told me she wanted to sell her apartment in London. "Well you should use my realtor! I just bumped into him not long ago, let me send you his contact info!" Sam ended up helping her sell her home and made a tidy commission, all because he was top of mind for me. When you stay active and update your network, and ask for future referrals, you will be the first person someone thinks of when they need the job done.

It can be helpful to mentally scroll through the last exchange you had with those who are important to you in business. Remember, it's human nature: even if you do ninety-nine things right, if you screw up the hundredth, that's what someone will remember. Harsh but true. On the other hand, you can use this to your advantage if you're generally reliable and you just happen to mess up once. Barrage the person with positives to wipe out the negative impression.

How to Leave a Job on Good Terms

1. Give ample notice: Two weeks is the norm, but be sensitive to timing. The more advance notice you can give your boss, the better.
2. Play it cool: Don't brag about your new job, and if you were let go (for good reason) then take it like an adult.
3. Say goodbye to your coworkers: After informing your boss, you should inform your coworkers. On your last day, send out the mass farewell email and cc your personal email so your coworkers can keep in touch.

4. Don't "check out" prematurely: Complete the tasks you are supposed to complete and wrap things up responsibly.

5. Offer to train your replacement: It shows a good attitude, your boss will love you for it, and it's the right thing to do.

6. Say good things: Practice the Chinese principle *hao lai hao qu* ("good come, good go"). It's a small world, and an especially small working world. Focus on your appreciation for the company and coworkers—you never know when one of them may be in a position to help or hinder your career in the future!

WORK: DIGITAL ETIQUETTE

In this era of changing work—where and when we do it, and what we expect to receive from it—it's easy to be lulled into informality. Keep in mind that business communication calls for a certain level of professionalism. We don't email or text our employers or even our colleagues as colloquially as we do our friends. As always, context is important.

Common Questions About Work Email

When should you write an email vs. call vs. visit face-to-face?
Writing an email is best for specific and mundane asks. But according to a *Harvard Business Review* study, face-to-face requests are thirty-four times more likely to garner positive responses than emails. For complex details and sensitive topics, where you have to judge the other person's reaction, make a phone call or meet face-to-face.

How should you start off and end emails?
I like to start off work emails with "Dear Zelda" or "Hi Zelda" followed by a comma. I don't use "good morning" or "good evening," as the time of day is not relevant to emails. End your email with "Kind regards, Sara." Other options are "All the best" or the British-inflected "Cheers." Or if it is a less formal conversation, then just your name.

What is the reasonable response time for an email?
Half your coworkers will expect a reply in under an hour. At the very least, emails should be replied to the same day or within twenty-four hours. The same goes for missed calls and texts. If someone hasn't replied in two days, you can follow up with a nudge—humans are humans, and they forget to reply when busy!

What is the etiquette on the use of "To" vs. "CC" vs. "BCC"?
Put everyone you want a response from in the To line. Save the CC (carbon copy) for those you want to keep looped in on the conversation but don't necessarily need a response from. BCC (blind carbon copy) is delicate. Only use it for mass emails or for following up when someone introduces you to someone else, in which case you move the original sender to bcc. When you email David and bcc Jenny, you're being dishonest by letting Jenny eavesdrop on your conversation. Be very careful, because Jenny might accidentally hit "Reply All," and then David could catch you!

What are the foolproof steps to sending an email?
Attach files first so you don't forget them, write the email body second, and add the email addresses last so as not to send them accidentally before you're ready. List emails in order of work title seniority.

Is it acceptable to send work emails late at night or on weekends?
Emails can be sent at any time, because it is up to the receiver to choose when to read them. That is what differentiates an email from a phone call or text message—technically it doesn't disturb anybody. On the other hand, you might want to think about what you're signaling if you send and receive work emails at all hours of the day and night.

What about exclamation points in emails?
It depends on the culture at your workplace, but even if they are accepted, use sparingly! Limit yourself to one exclamation mark per email! Otherwise you risk sounding upset or overeager!

What Do You Do If You Send a Text to or CC the Wrong Person?

Try not to panic. You need to think straight while you try to use the "unsend" feature on your phone or email app. There might still be time! Make sure in a calm moment to choose the maximum time frame for withdrawing a message. On Gmail, for example, you can extend the cancellation period from five seconds to thirty. That can feel like an eternity, but it might someday be long enough to save your skin. Just keep in mind that some "unsend" features, such as in Outlook, inform the recipient that you have tried to do so—even if the attempt was unsuccessful.

If it's too late, you have a couple of options: go off the grid permanently for the rest of your life, or quickly own up to your mistake. Depending on the circumstances, either abject remorse (see "Master the Art of the Apology," page 101) or humor will be the right way to go. Early in my investment banking career, I was the beneficiary of the latter approach when I made one of these heart-sinking mistakes.

An email arrived from a friend at Morgan Stanley one Sunday morning as I was sitting in my cubicle at Perella Weinberg. I had a couple of friends who were working at different banks, and we were always zipping each other emails. This one said, "Hey guys, free to have dinner tonight? It's my birthday," so I wrote back and said, "I'd love to join but can we make it in Midtown East and on the later side for those of us who unfortunately have to work on Sundays?" I added a few more members of our crew in the reply, including Peter Zhou. About thirty seconds later, I got a phone call from my friend Geoffrey: "Sara! You copied Peter Weinberg instead of our Peter!" To understand how I felt at that moment, you have to know not only that Peter Weinberg was the cofounder of the company I worked for but also that his name was practically synonymous with Goldman Sachs for decades and that he was incredibly courtly and dignified. I tried to recall the message on Outlook, but it was too late. Now he would see both the message *and* that I had tried to recall it. My stomach was knotted with dread. A few minutes later, I received a reply from him. "Hey, Sara, I want to go too! :)." Incredible relief washed over me. His use of kindly humor completely transformed what could have been a very sticky situation. Next time I saw him, I felt very sheepish, but he brushed away my concern with a smile.

The lesson? It's not the end of the world, even if you wish the earth would open up and swallow you. Apologize or make a joke, but regain your perspective as quickly as possible.

WORK: FAQ

Any recommendation on navigating business casual dress code now that we're all used to working from home?

I'm so glad you asked this question. Because everyone looks bad in business casual, it's all the more important to get it right. The boundaries are blurring between business casual and what has traditionally been called "smart casual," but essentially you can get away with anything that's fitted (not too tight or too baggy) so long as it's not a T-shirt or jeans, or flip-flops, or yoga pants, or shorts.

Are sneakers appropriate for casual work attire?

Only if they are leather (or vegan leather, of course).

Do I have to say good morning to every coworker I pass?

At the very minimum, make eye contact and smile.

What do I do when introducing two coworkers who are meeting for the first time?

As with social situations, you turn to the more senior or important person first (e.g., "Chairman Buffet, this is my assistant, Ben"). If they are equals, turn to the one you know less well and introduce your more familiar colleague to them.

What is the protocol on elevators? Do you exit and hold the door for others, or just exit and leave? Do you let women get off first, even if they're in the back?

Apply the accounting principle LIFO (last in, first out) to elevator etiquette. In work situations, gender doesn't apply. If you want to look respectful, especially toward a superior or client, make a show of holding your hand against the door on the way out.

What is a good opening question for a business acquaintance or potential client?

One of my favorite openers is, "What are you excited about these days?" It's an open question that can't be answered with a simple yes or no and provides an excellent opportunity to gather intelligence and allow the other person to open up.

I want to reach out to an acquaintance I haven't seen in a while to ask for career advice. I heard that his father died since we last spoke, and he is really struggling. Should I bring up what happened even though we are not close?

It is never too late to offer condolences. Reach out for the real reason—career advice—but when you speak, say your condolences up front to show the importance of his loss. "I just heard about your loss. I'm so sorry." Short, simple, and kind. Wait a beat or two to show respect before launching into the business part of the call.

What is the right amount of personal information to share at work?

Pro Tip: The amount of personal information to share at work depends on the generation. Millennials and Gen Z have very different expectations, with older colleagues finding it inappropriate to share your personal life and younger colleagues finding it inappropriate to conceal. The happy medium is to share just enough about yourself in order to be authentic, without getting too deep or making yourself too vulnerable. You will be happier and more satisfied with your work when you feel you can be yourself, but we have different "selves" in different contexts.

How to avoid coworkers that gossip?

Everybody loves to hear gossip. You don't want to be a Goody Two-shoes, or nobody is going to give you intel. On the other hand, don't chime in and say anything you could be held accountable for. Be careful what you post on social media, don't sleep with coworkers, and don't overshare, and you should be safe from being a target yourself.

Do you have any tips for women trying to get ahead about how not to get emotional in a meeting or confrontation? I work in energy, a very male-dominated industry where situations inherently induce frustration or anger, but showing that—even accidentally—just skewers your reputation.

When you feel like your emotions are overwhelming you or you might cry at work, focus on a tiny detail. If you're in a meeting, for example, concentrate on your pen. Focus on the tip or the brand name. If you're face-to-face with someone, pick out a detail of their clothing, like their tie. Or even a mole on their neck. Just don't look at their eyes.

Block out other thoughts. When you zoom in on a tiny detail, you go into a form of meditation and transcend your emotions.

We have one Black employee on the team. How to celebrate her without singling her out?

It is important to celebrate diversity, but it's not fair to expect minority groups—whether that's gender, sexual orientation, race, or ethnicity—to represent their entire community. You might feel as if you're helping your colleague to be "seen," but chances are she just wants to be able to do her job successfully, like everybody else. Be sensitive to any cues that she's having difficulties, but other than that, her competence will be "celebration" enough.

How do I say no to a coworker who asks for my help?

If it's something you're not knowledgeable about, you can say, "I'm not the best person to ask since this isn't my area of expertise, but you know who can **really** *help you here? David."*

If you're too busy, be honest! Say, "Unfortunately, I'm swamped with deadlines right now, but you know who seems to be pretty free recently? David. Maybe he would have more time to help you out." In either case, make sure it's true.

My colleague is always having personal conversations at her desk. How do I tell her it's disruptive?

Point Ms. Talkative to a quiet nook or staff kitchen.

Is it okay to fart in the elevator if no one else is in it?

Yes, because you're alone. But it would be embarrassing if someone you knew walked in after you. (The same goes for doing a number two in the office restroom stall.)

Is it okay to sleep with my boss?

Only if they're the last person you ever sleep with . . .

A colleague just stole my idea. What should I do?

How good is your self-control? Time spent trying to control the behavior of a guilty colleague is time wasted. Console yourself with the fact that your colleague had to resort to cheating to get ahead. If you complain to your supervisor, you'll look like you're still in high school. Take the high road and leave it to karma.

How do you professionally say "Kiss my ass"?

By saying nothing. Don't validate.

What are your thoughts on dressing better than your manager or seniors?

Don't have a more expensive watch than your boss. If they are not well dressed, keep your look understated. You don't want to be in a meeting where the client mistakes you for the boss. If they are impeccably put together, then emulate—people like it when their staff look the part. A friend of mine shared a story about mimicking her boss's style when she was an assistant at a publishing house. One day, she heard her boss exclaim delightedly to another department head, "Isn't it adorable? She dresses just like me!" My friend was promoted a few months later.

How do I discuss my "side hustle" business with my colleagues?

You don't. You never want to give your colleagues ammunition to use against you if things should go sour in the future, and showing that you're not 100 percent invested in the company (even if it's true) is like exposing your jugular.

PART THREE

DATING AND RELATIONSHIPS

*My alone feels so good . . . I'll only have
you if you're sweeter than my solitude.*

—WARSAN SHIRE

Love does not dominate; it cultivates.

—JOHANN WOLFGANG VON GOETHE

Your Best Self in Love

Work is where we present our public face. Our work self doesn't change much over time and depends mainly on the setting we're in, not the person or people we're with. But in our love relationships, it is just the opposite. The decision about whether to bare our innermost selves is purely personal, and even the term "falling in love" captures how much change we undergo in the journey from stranger to soulmate. But since passion clouds our judgment, bad behavior is almost inevitable. That's where etiquette comes in.

Part of what usually keeps us well-behaved is the knowledge that others are watching. In our romantic lives, however, almost everything happens behind closed doors. All too often, people confuse privacy with permission to act out and hurt each other. That is why we need etiquette. Etiquette is not ethics, but the tools it provides serve as guardrails to protect you (and others) as you put your best self forward from the first date onward.

The Third Secret of Social Fluency: Empathy

The next secret of social fluency is being able to interact with others in an empathetic way. How can you maintain your self-esteem along with that of everyone concerned in today's sometimes exhausting and demoralizing dating and relationship arena? Be the change you want to see.

In case this sounds saccharine, let me clarify that empathy is commonly misunderstood. Rather than sympathy on steroids, or a hypersensitive tendency to absorb and actually feel other people's pain, empathy is not about feelings at all. It is a mental exercise that involves putting yourself in someone else's shoes to imagine how *they* are feeling, not how you would be feeling in their situation. That's an important distinction.

Gary Noesner, the former chief of the FBI's Crisis Negotiation Unit, put it this way: "It's not sympathy. It's not agreement, and it requires no common ground." Empathy is a tool for creating a rapport with another person, a two-way street for communication. Noesner developed the FBI's seven active listening skills to deal with hostage negotiations. If empathy works in that situation, it should work to defuse an overheated argument with a loved one. Here are the steps, with role-play dialogue you might generate if you were hearing about this for the first time.

1. **Offer minimal encouragements:** "Uh huh, yes, I see."
2. **Paraphrase:** "So you're saying that sympathy is not the same as empathy."
3. **Label emotions:** "I sense that you're feeling impatient with this discussion and want me to get to the useful tips."
4. **Try mirroring** (repeating the last few words of the speaker's sentence): "the useful tips."
5. **Ask open-ended questions:** "And how would you use these techniques in a relationship situation?"
6. **Use "I" messages:** "I feel pressured because I'm never going to remember all of these suggestions."
7. **And effective pauses:** ". . ."

I learned most about empathy from my first serious boyfriend, Jesse, whom I dated in business school. He was a man's man who was also caring and sensitive to others' feelings—and secure enough to reach out and express his own. Whenever I was upset or excited, he would try to put himself in my shoes and imagine how I felt. For example, when I was elated at finishing my last exam of the semester, he beamed, "You must feel so happy and liberated!" When I was dejected about a conflict I had with a friend, he said, "I'm sorry you're going through this. I can't even imagine how disappointed you must feel." It was strange and wonderful to receive acknowledgment without judgment, especially having been raised by a Chinese Tiger Mother for whom empathy was a foreign concept.

I have since tried to put what I learned from Jesse to good use, becoming a kinder and more understanding friend to my friends, teacher to my students, and wife to my husband. In *Mind Your Manners*, my students had all sorts of personal and familial anguish that warped their perspective and led them to do surprising things. When they confided in me, I tried to acknowledge and share their feelings without showing judgment. Empathy is the most loving tool you can ever use to achieve success in every area of your life, from friendship and romance to work and family.

If They Don't Give You a Time, You Don't Have a Date

It's frustrating to flirt with somebody (by text or in the flesh) who gets your hopes up but doesn't follow through with making plans. It's worse if they suddenly pop up with a late-night text asking if you're still up. Unless you're down with being a booty call, the best response is none at all.

When I was around thirty and looking for a serious relationship, I played a lot of message tag with a guy named Chris. He hadn't asked me out on a date, but we were clearly interested in each other. I was excited when he sent me a text saying, "let's find a time next week to meet up," but I was unpleasantly surprised when he followed up a few nights later a little before 10 p.m. with "i'm at a bar near your house." I thought about replying, but I realized there was really nothing to say. I waited till the next morning and said I had already gone to sleep. I'm all for spontaneity, but not before any sort of relationship has been established. That was the end of Chris as far as I was concerned. People reveal themselves early. NB: This doesn't apply to a platonic friend of course. But if you are seriously interested in dating the person, train them to plan ahead of time with you.

Dating Apps 101

Now that we're told heterosexual couples are more likely to meet online than through friends and connections, a handy cheat sheet of the rules would be nice.

1. **Your profile photo should be recent and recognizably you.** No one likes a bait and switch.
2. **Let your friends (preferably of your target market) choose your profile photo.** Studies show this approach yields better success than choosing it yourself.
3. **And make sure you smile and face forward.** These increase your chances of being swiped right by 14 percent and 20 percent, respectively.
4. **More is more. Be detailed, specific, and honest when describing yourself and your interests.** Word pictures are important too.

5. **Save the small talk for real life.** Skip those empty exchanges online that start boring and lead nowhere. Those people are wasting your precious time.
6. **Always meet for the first time in public.** Safety first.
7. **Take your own transportation.** Ditto.
8. **The biggest online turnoff is sexual innuendo.** In real life, it's getting too drunk.
9. **Other deal-breakers?** Constantly checking your phone on a date and immediately adding someone on social media.
10. **As Brené Brown says**, "Clear is kind. Unclear is unkind." It's better to be upfront quickly if you know things aren't going to work out.

Admitting Vulnerability Is the First Step to Intimacy

Unlike most of my American friends, I started dating late. Even from halfway around the world, my Tiger Mom made sure I didn't allow boys to take my focus off my studies—and it's true that even in college my grades would nose-dive whenever I had a crush on someone. More generally, I was on my own and self-sufficient from an early age, and it was a point of pride that I didn't need to depend on anyone else. I even discouraged my parents from flying over to help me move into Georgetown when I was a seventeen-year-old freshman. I wanted to spare them the jet lag from the tortuous and torturous journey. They were supportive in a distant sort of way, but—like many Chinese parents and children—intimacy wasn't a feature of our relationship.

All this is to say that I didn't start dating until I arrived in

New York City at twenty-one. Sara Jane the party girl was finally allowed out, but I wouldn't say that I had emotionally satisfying relationships. It was very important for me to stay noncommittal and never say out loud that I liked someone, even if I did. Always having the upper hand was a badge of honor. My first wake-up call that this was not a sign of strength was Germain, an early memorable relationship at business school.

Germain was French and incredibly charming. He was in my section, a group of approximately ninety students with whom we spent our first-year curriculum, and we had intense chemistry over the course of the first few weeks of class. We were hanging out one day when he said, "You're not like other girls." When I asked him what he meant, he said, "They'd say, 'What do you think of me? Do you like me? What are we?'" But I hadn't asked any of that. A bell went off in my head. Really? That's what they do? It was a revelation that emotionally healthy people would admit that they cared about each other rather than withhold in order to maintain a power position. Things ended up not working out between Germain and me, but I had learned a vital lesson.

In retrospect, I see that the wonderful marriage I'm in today was made possible by the revelation I had all those years ago. The takeaway? Be vulnerable, and be upfront about stating what kind of relationship you want from the start. You'll save yourself a lot of time and heartache.

Don't Mention or Ask About Exes Until Your Third Date

Ah, the temptation. Is there anything more delicious than unloading about your ex? What is more satisfying than describing the villain who ruined your life, who is the reason you're sitting here on this date in the first place when you are so irresistible? The need to explain ourselves, to tell our own side of the story, to wallow delicately in self-pity while denying that's what we're doing, these are the less desirable traits of human nature. Refrain from displaying them, at least until they've seen some of your better qualities! And beware of the converse: if he starts describing his crazy ex, take a closer look at him.

You can and should, however, ask about their relationship experience by the third date. Date three is when you should make a decision about whether a relationship is worth pursuing. Aside from not wasting your own time, if you're going out with people older than you, it's important to at least know they're not married.

The question "Have you ever been married?" is worded carefully to catch the not-as-rare-as-you-would-hope person who is currently married! Do I need to pause here and say that "We're married in name only" means they're married? As does "We're separated," and "I'm going through the process of divorce." This last answer my friend Camilla got on her third date with William, a stunningly attractive man she'd had a fling with right before she broke up with a long-term abusive boyfriend for good. Camilla was honest with William in return, and they both decided the sexual attraction was too strong to resist. No judgment, I'm just saying we should be informed consumers. Camilla and William knew exactly what they were (and were not) getting into, and not only was it the hottest two weeks Camilla ever spent, but it also helped give her the strength to get out of that toxic relationship.

Wait Until You Can't Stand It Anymore to Have Sex—It Will Be Even Better

Yes, I know. There are starkly conflicting opinions about this issue. Some advice-givers say it doesn't matter if you have sex on (or even before!) the first date; others say to wait a prescribed number of times (two, three, six, and beyond). But the fact is that when libido (plus alcohol) is involved, outcomes are unpredictable. Unless you know in advance that you're in it solely for a quick bit of fun, I suggest waiting as long as you can for a few reasons.

First, and most importantly, we all want to protect our delicate feelings (and precious bodies) from hookups that aren't going to offer us anything and might even leave us feeling worse afterward. So, if you can take it or leave it, leave it. Secondly, once we have sex, where is there left to go? Human beings (which include heterosexual males) are often creatures who get off on the chase. Once they've caught you, the thrill is gone, so make sure something else is in place to compensate for what's lost in excitement. When I wanted to be serious, I always waited for the man to profess his love and commitment before having sex. Thirdly, and most importantly, waiting is a good idea because the rush of hormones produced during sex creates feelings of attachment before you have time to figure out whether or not someone is good for you. Sexual chemistry doesn't necessarily equal compatibility.

When You're Nervous, Slow Your Movements (Including the Ones Your Lips Are Making)

Some of us talk a lot when we're tense, and our nervous chatter can look like insecurity to those who clam up when socially anxious. If you're prone to speak fast when you're ill at ease, you might notice that your gestures speed up as well. Therefore, an easy and effective way to appear more confident is to slow your speech and movements. Exaggerate how slowly you respond (both your response time and your speech itself). Move as if you are underwater and you'll be surprised at how much more in control you feel. And don't forget to breathe!

If You Find You're Talking a Lot, Ask Yourself, "When Was the Last Time I Asked a Question?"

The 20-second rule (p. 109) applies here in spades. That's how long you can speak uninterrupted before you hit a conversational yellow light. Don't get so drunk on self-revelation that you forget yourself. They're called conversation *partners* for a reason. One important point to remember if you're on the receiving end of a flood of self-revelation on a first date: some people go on and on about themselves not because they're narcissistic (although that's possible) but because they don't usually get a chance to open up. Suddenly finding themselves across the table from an attractive prospect can open the floodgates. So, give them a chance if they seem nice otherwise, and try to manage the conversation back to topics of mutual interest. If they persist, though, they might actually be self-involved.

> It's okay to disappear after one date.
> If you're tempted to explain why you don't want to see them again, you might make them feel worse.
> If you're on the receiving end, take the hint and be grateful.

Once You Know You Like Someone, Deactivate Your Dating Apps

There is such a thing as too much choice. The more options we have, the more we stress over making the right decision and the less likely we are to feel we have chosen correctly. The secret to happiness is to realize that perfection does not exist. There is such a thing as "good enough." Dating is no exception.

By voluntarily drawing the line—and deactivating your dating apps—when you find someone you care about, you will increase your chances of happiness. As tempting as it is to seek validation of your current partner while preserving the fantasy of an alternative future with a different one, you can't have your cake and eat it too.

I've known my friend Amy for nine years; she's thirty-nine and gorgeous, a real badass when it comes to business. When it comes to men, however, she is incredibly avoidant. Although she married once and divorced when she was younger, she's since been with a series of noncommittal guys who aren't nearly as impressive as she is. As her armor, she likes to play the field, and her way of protecting herself is to diminish how important the guy of the moment is to her by keeping another in the wings. She's already out even while she's in.

I'd never known her to be in a serious relationship until she met Everett last summer on OkCupid. She clearly likes him, and he's a fellow neuroscience nerd, which is not easy to find. More importantly, he is a solid, straightforward guy, and securely attached. He is so dependable that she calls him her "rock." So I was surprised, early on, when she was on the fence because some of her friends thought he was boring. "Are you kidding?" I said. "Who's going out with him, you or them?"

I was surprised once again a while later when she asked, "Do you think I should delete my dating apps? I noticed that Everett already deleted his." They'd been seeing each other exclusively for two or three months by then. "Of course you should," I said, a little too sharply. "But what if this doesn't work out?" she asked. "It would only take a minute to download them again," I replied, "but in the meantime imagine how he would feel if he saw them on your phone." She shook her head. I pressed my point. "Amy, it's about time you align your head and your heart. I'd say the only person you're hurting is yourself, but that's not true anymore." I don't know if it was my stubbornness or if a little light bulb went off in her head, but she deleted them on the spot. I'm happy to say she and Everett are still going strong.

We all know people who behave like this. You might be one of them yourself. Usually this misalignment between head and heart results from some trauma in the past, which is why I'm such a big advocate of therapy. But when you find something good, seize it with both hands (after you delete those apps).

Early in Love, Break a Date or Say No to Something to See How the Person Responds

Raishel Jones, from Episode 3 of *Mind Your Manners*, was raised by her aunts (her mother's sisters). As we shared love and dating tips during the dumpling-making session with other students, she volunteered this nugget of pure gold from her aunts. Early in a relationship, break a date or say no to something and gauge the person's reaction. Unfortunately, that scene didn't make the final cut, but as a dating diagnostic tool, it's unparalleled!

I wish I had known this tip years ago. Matthew, the guy I infamously broke up with over text, would not accept no for an answer. He often became angry and petulant when I tried to change plans. What this meant was that he had no respect for my boundaries. If he behaved this way over small things, I should have known how he would explode over larger issues down the road. It was always his way or the highway.

Another diagnostic tool is how your date treats servers, sales-people, and Uber drivers. Matthew would always dress down and yell at anyone in a service position. I was embarrassed to go to restaurants with him, especially when I knew the owner. By con-trast, on one of my early dates with my now husband, when a wait-ress spilled soup all over his expensive jacket he was unfazed and just patted away at it casually, as though nothing had happened.

If You Can't Choose Wisely, Cut Quickly

Forgive a girl a little economics talk, but let's discuss the sunk-cost fallacy. Continuing with something even when it is not beneficial or desirable simply because of the resources that have already been invested in it is a common but costly mistake. This applies to sticking with a poor investment, finishing a boring book, or pur-suing a dead-end relationship. Economists, who understand the concept of sunk costs far better than most people, often choose to leave bad movies or stop eating a bad meal rather than continuing just because they invested in it. The rest of us, however, find it difficult to get this message through our heads.

Take my former student Michelle. In her early thirties, beauti-ful, and very sweet, she was a yoga teacher when she first took my class. I soon inspired her to start her own yoga studio, introducing her to a designer and other contacts she needed. About a month after she graduated, we had a friendly lunch to touch base. She confided that she was stuck in a rut relationship with her boyfriend. They had been living together, but neither was interested in getting married. She was far from excited about the relationship; if anything, I got the sense that he was dragging her down a bit. But she bemoaned wasting the six years she had already "invested" in the relationship.

I didn't bother trying to correct her thinking, but in true Sara Jane Ho style, I told her to move out. "You don't have to break up right away if that's too much for you," I said, "but get your own place." Next, I told her to enroll in an Executive MBA program as she felt she was out of her league now that she was managing a team of a dozen people. "That's what an Executive MBA is for, after all," I told her, "people who already have management roles and need to learn some skills. Plus," I added with a smile, "they'll all be older, successful people, mostly men, and you might meet your next boyfriend there. Then if you want, you can break up with your current boyfriend." And that's exactly what happened! When I spoke to her a year later, she shared that she was married and having a baby!

If Michelle had continued to be seduced by the sunk-cost fallacy, she'd still be living in a dead-end situation. The essential point is that *you can't get back the time, money, effort, or emotion you invested in the past*. The past is irrelevant when making a decision. Look to the future instead.

There's No Such Thing as the Right Time to Break Up with Someone

The *New York Times* titled my Style profile, "The Etiquette Guru Who Broke Up with a Boyfriend over Text," so I definitely know what I'm talking about here! I was deep into the second week of filming *Mind Your Manners* when I had an epiphany. How could I justifiably tell other people how to live their best lives after spending multiple evenings crying on the phone with my boyfriend? The cognitive dissonance was so strong that it made me feel like a hypocrite. My relationship with Matthew had made me doubt and second-guess myself for four years. Was I going to let it ruin my one chance to film a Netflix special too? In the harsh sunlight of Sydney, Australia, my choice was suddenly clear. As the car pulled up to my student Stephanie Osifo's house, I sent off a text message to him that read, "I can't be showing up on set with red and puffy eyes because you're making me cry." We had discussed breaking up many times throughout our relationship, but this time felt different. I knew it was final, and I felt free.

> "Tell me, what is it you plan to do with your one wild and precious life?"
>
> —MARY OLIVER,
> "THE SUMMER DAY"

I can't resist adding that his ex-wife asked him for a divorce by email—and cc'd his mother.

Everything is contextual. Breaking off a long-term relationship by text was not strictly correct, but it was right for me. If you're in a relationship that you know is wrong, any time is the right time to break up.

Feng Shui for Love

When you ask for something better, new space needs to be created for a fresh start. To find new

love in your life, clear away any physical reminders that no longer serve you.

Give away gifts/mementos/anything that reminds you of an ex: there are karmic implications. Remove negative symbolism; keep photos and artwork pleasing, inspiring, and uplifting.

Leave room for someone. If you want a relationship, do not have a single bed. Use a double bed, and do not push your bed against the wall. It should have space to breathe and enter from both sides. Same for your closet—leave space for another person to enter your life.

If you want to start a relationship, don't surround yourself with single imagery—add doubles to every room. Create an energy of partnership around you—a pair of stools, a pair of chairs, a pair of nightstands, a pair of lamps. Your bedroom setup should be symmetrical.

Use pink to attract love and romance, and red to solidify an existing relationship. No mirror facing the bed—it will mean a third party interferes.

If a Friend Is Dating Someone You Have Serious Reservations About, You Have One Chance to Tell Them So—and It Can Only Be Your Bestie

Ideally, you should share your worries soon after you meet the person, but sometimes your objections will stem from information you get once the relationship is established—alcohol or drug abuse, for example, or infidelity. In that case, you should approach your friend as quickly as you can after learning the worrisome news; otherwise, they will suspect you have been harboring suspicions or even talking about them behind their back, which will poison your friendship. You want to be as matter-of-fact as possible. Don't be mean, but don't beat around the bush either. It's a bit of a tightrope. Since this is your one chance, you don't want to squander it; nor do you want to ruin your bestie relationship.

Rehearse what you are going to say, making sure to include specific examples of the behavior that worries you. Don't just make vague generalizations (e.g., Don't say, "He doesn't seem very nice"). If you've observed him making nasty comments, write them down and quote them back to your friend as evidence. Also try to come up with responses to any possible objections you can foresee. If he has been unemployed for two years in a good labor market, for example, and has moved into your friend's apartment rent-free, try to anticipate what excuses your friend will make for the new living arrangement. Above all, stay calm!

I was on the receiving end of one of these "interventions" a few years ago. I'd been dating Matthew for about a year when he met my friends Olivier and Mike. They treat me like a bro, and we share a lot of laughs together. We were having lunch in a Beijing food court, and they were checking out girls on Tinder. A lot of jokes and jabs were traded back and forth concerning my friends' single status and dating adventures, but Matthew had no sense of humor and didn't join in. Being an adventurous eater, he had ordered a bowl of bull penis noodles, a somewhat unusual dish even in China! Even though the dish only cost five dollars, he was complaining there wasn't enough penis in it. He went on and on for so long that I finally told him to get over it, but he wouldn't stop. Worse, he didn't see the humor of complaining that there wasn't enough penis in his noodles. My friends were becoming more and more raucous, and it was clear he wasn't fitting in.

The next time I saw Olivier, we had dinner alone, and as soon as we sat down at the restaurant he said, "Honey, you've *got* to break up with your boyfriend. He has no sense of humor. And you're not yourself around him." That last point was the most important. I came up with some weak defenses, but deep down I knew he was right. I did, however, continue to date Matthew for three more years. I didn't see Olivier very much during that period, though, because my boyfriend didn't like him. To be more specific, he was really jealous of Olivier and how much he made me laugh. He was convinced that there had been something between us in the past, which wasn't true.

After I finally broke up with Matthew, Olivier said, "You know how I feel about him, right?" He managed to restrain himself from saying I told you so, which was commendable. When you're proven right, bite your tongue and just be happy your friend finally saw the light. And remember, once you have your say, mum's the word.

You Teach People How to Treat You

The process of teaching others how to treat us begins the moment we meet. People take us at our own estimation. What other information do they have? Demand respect, and people will give it to you—unless you give them a specific reason not to. Our relationships are a continual feedback loop. Every action elicits a reaction. And every reaction provides information that alters the next action. If someone behaves well and we reward them for it, they will continue to do so. If they behave well and we take it for granted, they have no incentive to keep making the effort. On the other hand, if someone violates our trust and we allow that to go unchallenged, they will continue the behavior. People are driven by self-interest, and if there are no consequences for pursuing their goals at our expense, they have no reason to rein themselves in. It seems almost painfully simple, yet it is a law we ignore at our own peril.

I had a somewhat spotty track record in this area when I met Jason, the man I would eventually marry. Fairly early in our relationship, he made arrangements to come to Shanghai and bring me back by train to his hometown for Chinese New Year. Three days before he was due to arrive, I asked him if he would be on time for dinner, since I was planning to cook for my godchildren and their parents. He wouldn't give me a straight answer. I asked him again the next day and got the same evasive response, getting more annoyed as I had to know how many to prepare for. Finally, four hours before the actual meal, I lost my patience and called him. "You say you want me to be your wife and you can't even commit to whether you'll be at a simple dinner? I'm a big girl. If you can't come, just say so, but stop with the in-between crap." He hastened to apologize and confessed that he was trying to avoid going into a hospital to get the COVID test required before boarding the train. Chinese people are very superstitious about doing anything in the fifteen days surrounding Chinese New Year as what happens in that period is supposed to set the tone for the entire year. I told him all he had to do was be honest with me, and he promised he would be clear from then on. He sent me a photo fifteen minutes later of himself on the train, and he has been true to his word ever since!

Playing the Victim Is a Role, Not a Reality

Training others can be hard work. Sometimes it is easier just to complain and play the victim—but I say "play the victim" because it is a role, not a reality. I had this realization about six months after I started therapy (my therapist, Theresa, is so wonderful that seven of my friends are now patients; we call her "Mother Theresa"). I had been set up with a guy named Paul who split his time between Taipei and Shanghai. One weekend when we were just starting to date, he said he was going to fly to Shanghai to visit me. When the day arrived, however, he didn't end up taking the flight. He was very odd and cagey on the phone, and it eventually became clear that he had been offended when he called the previous day and I wasn't very responsive because I was busy teaching. Not coming was his way of getting back at me.

I had a therapy session that day, and I was feeling very shaky and insecure after my conversation with Paul. Theresa asked, "What are you looking for in a relationship?" As I started listing all the things I wanted—someone to make me feel safe and secure, someone who would never intentionally hurt me—it hit me. Paul was not someone I wanted to spend my time and energy on. I can't remember exactly what message I texted him, but the gist of it was that his behavior wasn't something I would tolerate in a relationship. I said we should just be friends, which I had no intention of doing, of course. It was so easy to step out of the victim role once the dynamic became clear, and I was proud of myself for nipping a potentially toxic relationship in the bud. As I said before, people reveal themselves early.

When it comes to unhealthy relationships, you can get out of the elevator at any floor, but some people like my friend Ada ride it all the way down to the basement. She often calls me to complain about a marketing exec she's sleeping with and how he refuses to commit to her. She bemoans how he blows hot and cold, messages her he loves her but then after she sleeps with him doesn't call her for weeks. And he has a terrible reputation as a cheater. She even saw him flirting with other girls online but didn't confront him. Finally, after two years of the same story, I lost my patience and told her, "The problem isn't this man. The problem is why YOU let him treat you this way." There was a silence on the phone. I went on, saying she should block him. "I can't do that," she said. "It would be rude!" How many times have I heard that? I suggested messaging in advance saying, "I can't do this anymore because the way you treat me is too painful. So I am going to delete you from my communication." She didn't do it, but the fact was that any self-respecting woman would have deleted him two years ago. The question was, why hadn't she? What happened in her past that was preventing her from treating herself with respect, and therefore preventing others from following suit? We've all been there. No matter man or woman, we've all been with someone who didn't treat us well. Many people have childhood traumas that affect their self-confidence, which is why I am a big proponent of therapy. It's better to address these problems early and maximize the years available to you for happiness.

> "The only difference between my friends who are in committed and happy relationships and those who are not is therapy."
>
> —MY FRIEND MASHA

The victim role is optional in business as well as personal affairs. When faced with a colleague who takes credit for your efforts, or a demanding boss who disregards your requests for fairness, ask yourself about the purpose and reward of such a dynamic. In every relationship, there is a balance of power and pleasure. To put it baldly: however painful the dynamic, if it's a pattern, you're getting something out of it. It may be painful to acknowledge this, particularly if it does not flatter your own character, but it's the only way to initiate change. Although the victim role might elicit sympathy and absolve you of responsibility, self-pity is not an attractive trait, nor is it likely to bring you closer to your goals. It's imperative to cast off the blindfold and be honest with yourself. A moment's embarrassment is a small price to pay to release yourself from a toxic spiral.

> Choosing how you want to live and how you want to be treated will give you more power than any material object ever could.

Only You Can Victimize Yourself

A forty-one-year-old friend of mine, Lily, told me about her relationship woes with a Danish guy she had been having casual sex with for two years. "You won't believe this," she said as we picked at a sushi platter between us. "Remember how we thought the Danish guy was a decent guy? A mutual friend of ours just told me that he has been married the whole time, and the wife and kid have been living in London!" I was shocked. "It's terrible that he hid this from you," I said. Then I paused and added, "Did you ever ask?" "No, I never asked," she replied, "and it really annoys me that everyone is telling me I should have, as though it's my fault!"

I was confused. I had been telling Lily for at least fifteen out of the twenty-four months she had been sleeping with the

Danish guy to ask him if he was exclusively seeing her, and that since she liked him, she should at least find out more about his relationship status or history. But for some reason she never brought herself to.

"Hang on, you've been sleeping with this guy who is in his midforties for two years on and off, and you haven't done any due diligence? If you haven't asked, it means you don't care, which makes me think you don't really have a right to be upset. I've asked you multiple times since you first slept with him, 'Why is he single at his age? Has he been married before, and is he seeing you exclusively?' It feels like I care more than you do! And now you're upset?"

Lily began to get defensive so I decided to switch the topic. "How's the Italian guy?" I asked, referring to a man in his midforties with whom she had also been having casual sex for the last two years. "After the way he two-timed you, I hope he's had the decency to finally leave you alone." She gave a guilty smile. "Well . . . actually . . . he saw my post that I'm moving away next week, so he messaged me to meet up." I put my chopsticks down.

"Wait, what?! He didn't respect you at all, had a fiancé part of the time, and broke your heart. Yet now he booty calls you, and you're going to drop everything and run over to him? You usually call me the next day saying you feel used! Don't tell me you're going to see him!" I said emphatically. She was.

Lily is my friend, but after twenty-four months of patiently explaining how these men were not good for her, and patiently lending my ear to her woes, that was the evening I privately decided I'd had enough of hearing about her victimizing herself. I joked that I didn't want to sound like a broken record and changed the topic.

Compare forty-one-year-old Lily with fourteen-year-old Annabelle, whose father asked me to take her out for a mentoring lunch. She told me about a boy she liked at school, so I teased, "Have you kissed yet?" "No," she replied, "I plan on asking him what he thinks of me before any of that stuff." I was struck by her self-confidence. Thoroughly impressed, I asked her why. "Because I don't want to feel bad doing all that stuff with him if he isn't serious about me." I hope my future daughter has the same self-respect.

Use "Soft Power" to Persuade

Etiquette is power, but it is soft power. The ability to make someone do what you want without their being aware of it sounds Machiavellian, but it is not—or not exactly. Soft power is not trickery; it is persuasion of the highest order. It has been said that while "hard"—or traditional—power can be equated with twisting someone's arm, "soft" power involves twisting their mind. If you want to change the way your partner dresses, for example, don't criticize. Instead, compliment them on something you want them to wear more of. For example, "This white jacket looks so good on you! Much better than that gray jacket you wore the other day."

Persuasion is all about communication, and being successful requires emotional intelligence. In order to be smooth rather than forceful, especially when there is conflict, you must first understand yourself and master your own emotions. Early on in my relationship with my husband, he said to me, "Let me tell you what kind of person I am in an argument. If you are hard, I will be harder. If you are soft, I will be softer." True to form, when we bickered the first time, over me keeping something from him, and I dug in my heels, he dug his in deeper. When we really reached an impasse, I thought to myself, *Do I want to be right or do I want to be happy? Maybe I should try listening to his hint.* I put aside my ego and said, "I'm sorry, it was insensitive of me. I should have informed you sooner instead of hiding it from you." He melted in front of my eyes, took the blame himself, and said, "My dear wife, there is no such thing as perfection. If you were perfect, then that would be your flaw!" and within seconds was back to his loving self. I was startled until I realized this particular trait is not unique to my husband. It applies to nearly everyone. It was just unique in that he communicated it to me, and he reminds me every time we have an argument that has the potential to get heated. Then I remember not to fight fire with fire. I reach for water instead.

Don't Twist Yourself into a Pretzel to Maintain a Connection

Drawing boundaries is as important in love as it is in work. Sometimes we automatically feel that we have to exchange our freedom for safety, but I've discovered it's possible to have both—if you set it up that way from the beginning. In her international bestseller *Mating in Captivity*, Esther Perel cautions against confusing love with merging. Even in established couples, she says, sexual attraction requires a degree of emotional separateness, i.e., boundaries.

Your partner fell in love with you for a reason. They liked what your life looked like when they met you. If you trade that away for some illusion of security, you diminish yourself *and* the relationship. So think about what is important to you and figure out how to safeguard it. It might be walking ten thousand steps a day, intermittent fasting, time alone to read or meditate, or socializing with your friends once a week. Some compromise will always be necessary, but if you sacrifice what makes you happy, you will end up asking for too much from your partner to compensate. Eventually, you will come to resent them.

If someone tries to cajole you into giving up what makes your life worthwhile, take heed. It's a sign of much more serious control issues down the road.

Don't Avoid Conflict—and When You Fight, Fight Fair

The conflict avoidant among us would rather have our fingernails pulled out than engage in a disagreement. The problem is that avoiding issues doesn't make them go away, for you or your partner. Psychologists call tucking all of your resentments away without dealing with them "gunnysacking." Once the sack gets too full of grievances, you explode, leaving devastation all around. Aha, you think, no wonder I don't like confrontation. You vow never to do it again, and the cycle starts all over again.

To have a healthy relationship, conflicts need to be aired and addressed. Many conflict avoiders grew up in circumstances where speaking up was traumatic or disagreements got out of hand, even violent. Others never saw their parents disagree and assumed that problems magically disappeared—until they went out into a world where that was patently untrue. Learning how to fight fair is not easy or simple, but there is a wealth of advice available. So do your research. Create a plan, stay calm, and have an exit strategy. Be brave enough to face disharmony when it arises rather than stuffing it into that gunnysack.

Once the conflict has been aired, however, don't let it spill over into your other interactions. One thing I observed in my own home growing up was that when my mother had an argument with my father (or me) she would sulk and let her pissy attitude carry over into our exchanges later in the day or even week. My dad never did, and it was always such a relief when he behaved normally about a neutral topic after we'd had a fight.

Allowing anger and resentment from previous conflicts to seep where it doesn't belong can be a relationship-ending flaw. A friend of mine in her twenties who dated an older man recounted that they had a stupid argument one morning about something she can't even remember. That evening, he called her from the side of the road with a flat tire in the pouring rain. Instead of being the friendly and supportive voice he longed to hear, she was sullen and hostile, still fuming from the earlier fight. He broke up with her the next day, calmly telling her that she was too immature for him, which she admits was probably true. But she did learn the valuable lesson of keeping anger within the bounds of the conflict where it belongs. You can disagree and still be loving.

> "Couples who laugh together, last together."
>
> —DR. JOHN GOTTMAN

Laughter Is an Aphrodisiac

We are all fallible, so it is a wonderful gift to have a partner who can gently tease you about your foibles—and who can accept gentle teasing in return. There's even a word for the joy of being laughed at: gelotophilia. (It only sounds like the love of ice cream!) The emphasis is on "gentle," of course. There's nothing more wounding than sarcastic "humor" designed to hit a sore spot while preserving plausible deniability. We've all heard, "But you're so sensitive! I was only kidding," from someone who

151

has just pierced us through the heart. The bottom line is that using humor to calm your partner in an argument is a great way to improve relationship satisfaction. This can take any form, whether a private joke, a silly face, or a funny story.

As far as sex is concerned, studies have shown that women who find their male partners funny report more attraction. I can certainly vouch for that. I love to laugh and find a sense of humor irresistible. To get more explicit, women who have funny partners have more and stronger orgasms; they also initiate sex more and have more sex overall. Unfortunately, we're told funny women do not have the same sexual effect on men, but as I said above, using humor to lower the temperature (in a good way) contributes to the success of a relationship.

Meeting the Parents (and Friends)

It's the big moment. Your partner is ready to introduce you to their parents. How should you behave? My advice is pretty simple. Dial everything down. Keep your words and behavior muted. Everything you say and do will be scrutinized so thoroughly that your words and gestures are amplified. If their worst criticism is, "He/she seems so quiet," be grateful. They will later revise their opinion as they get to know you better. On the other hand, there's no way to undo overdoing it.

Dialing it down does not necessarily apply, however, when you meet a new partner's friends. Whether your partner realizes it or not, they are testing you. Do you stick by their side the whole time, or go off independently and mingle? Do you stay and have a great time, or whisper in their ear that you want to go home? They are observing and judging whether you are the right partner for them. And so are all of their friends. But hey, no pressure! Just relax and have fun.

When it comes to meeting your partner's friends for the first time, take the back seat and let your partner drive. But make sure to ride along at the same tempo. In Chinese we would say that you need to be like running water, flowing smoothly through the cracks. You don't want to be the downer girlfriend or boyfriend who looks unhappy, nor do you want to be an overly rambunctious attention seeker. You want to fit right in, as though you were made for their group all along.

The first time my husband met a big group of my friends was a month into our relationship. One Friday night, we were at my apartment in Shanghai when I received a message at 11:19 p.m. from my friend Ed. His message began with a group selfie, followed by "We are all so curious about your new boyfriend. Would you like to bring him out and join . . . ? We are at the Edition Hotel and realize we all know you. It's my birthday in one hour so come play."

Let me pull back and give some context. If this had happened with my *previous* boyfriend, Matthew, he would have immediately turned suspicious, saying, "Who is this guy? Why is he texting you so late at night? I've never heard you mention Ed before. What does he do? How do you know him? What message are you sending by going over so late at night?" And after a thirty-minute Spanish Inquisition, he would have sat back and said, "No, I don't feel like going." Which meant that there was definitely no chance he would let me go either.

With a deep breath and not knowing what to expect, I read the text aloud. "My friends are curious to meet you. Want to go?" I asked. He looked at me and smiled. "If you want to go, then I'll go. If you don't want to go, then I won't go." *Why is life with this man so easy?* I asked myself. As we left the house, he grabbed a limited edition of Maotai liquor, the most coveted alcohol in China. "That's going to be wasted on my Hong Kong friends," I said. "Save it for entertaining your government officials." "It's your friend's birthday, right?" he said. "Don't be cheap."

We showed up just before midnight at the hotel to find a group of a dozen people—mostly men, including some young men who'd graduated a few years behind me from Harvard Business School. When introducing new partners to my friends, I am always sure to stay by their side and facilitate introductions that serve as launchpads into interesting conversation, and to make sure they don't feel neglected. My one-month boyfriend bounced off and began downing shots with the other men, who were at least fifteen years younger than him. The only time he bounced back to find me was to remind me to serve Maotai to the others, who were duly impressed. It was a rousing and rowdy success.

At two a.m., when I was ready to leave, I yelled, "Babe, let's go home!" And he playfully retorted, "I don't want to!" When my friends laughed, I was astounded. It was a very high EQ move. Usually in big groups, we are quick to judge partners who drag our friends home unwillingly. We label that person a Debbie Downer. So he was making an impression that he was having such a good time that he didn't want to leave; he *really* fit in.

Find Out Their Family Dynamics—and How Their Parents Treat Each Other—Before You're in Too Deep

There's an old saying that men treat their girlfriends the way they treat their mothers. Whether or not that's true, both men and women are likely to treat their partners the way their parents treated each other. For that reason, it is certainly worth looking into the family dynamics of anyone you are seriously dating. I speak from painful experience, which I share in the hope that it might save someone from going through what I did.

Alan and I originally met through mutual friends when we were teenagers, but we both went off to study in the States and didn't start dating until I was twenty-eight. Like me, he had been raised in Hong Kong and studied in the US. When he returned to Hong Kong to do finance, he really swept me off my feet. He was charming, handsome, and a lot of fun. I was living in Beijing at the time and traveling back and forth to Hong Kong to date him, but I should have seen it as a warning sign that he wanted to get serious so quickly.

Another warning sign should have been his family history. His mother, who used to be a teacher at the American international school he attended, had major anger issues. When he was younger, she verbally and physically lashed out at him and his sister. Her husband was a timid shadow of a person who couldn't manage to stammer out a complete sentence. (Later, a girlfriend of mine who grew up in Alan's building told me that neighbors regularly called the police to report sounds of violence at their apartment.)

Two weeks into dating, Alan told me he was going to quit his job in Hong Kong and move to Beijing for me, and two months later he moved in with me there. While there were some red flags before that I had ignored, this was when I saw a truly ugly side of him. First, he became verbally abusive. Then he began to break things when angry. At breakfast one morning, he swept a bowl off the table with such force that it shattered on the wall behind my head. He blamed me, saying, "I did this because *you* provoked me." He began to threaten—"I'm going to break all the art in this

155

apartment." When I tried to leave, he confiscated my phone and locked me in a room.

On the outside, we were in a whirlwind eight-month romance, deeply in love, and on our way to getting engaged. Inside, I was terrified. Things were escalating in a scary way, and I could feel that the next step was physical violence. I knew that if I didn't get out now, I never would. The problem with abusers, however, is that they won't let you break up with them—at least not without a struggle.

I tried to get him to move out but he refused, so I staged my own intervention. I asked my housekeeper to hide my passport and ID to keep them safe, and in the meantime I invited both sets of parents to Beijing so I could break up with him there and have them take him back to Hong Kong immediately. My dad was in on the plan, but his parents had to be given the pretext that I was unwell and needed family support. Once they were there, I took his mother aside and said, "I'm not going to tell you every bad thing Alan has done to me. You've told me you know your son's anger issues and I'm just asking you woman to woman: How would you feel if your daughter was treated like this in a relationship? Please take him back to Hong Kong because I can't be with him anymore." Thank heavens it worked. I am still grateful for my narrow escape!

The interesting thing, though, was that after I broke up with him, his friends all came out of the woodwork. "We're so happy you're free of him. Did you know that his girlfriend from high school, whom he dated through college at NYU, had to go to the hospital because he physically abused her?" When I asked them why they hadn't told me before, I got the same response I got when I asked my cousin Gerran the same question: "You guys seemed so in love and so happy. I thought he might have changed.

And it's hard, you know . . . ?" He trailed off. No, I don't know. If someone has a history of being an abuser, and your relative or close friend is dating them, you should share it. Say, "This is vital information." You want the person to make an informed decision.

I wish someone had said something to me. Would I have acted faster? I don't know. But I hate to think about the possibility that I might not have acted at all. If you're in a similar situation, there are domestic violence hotlines available where you can find free and immediate help.

Reference Check Anyone You Are About to Be Serious with, Especially If You're Thinking of Marrying Them

A long-term relationship is like a business partnership—a marriage certainly is—but very few of us treat it like one. We fail to exercise even the most basic due diligence we'd use before choosing an employer, for example. It's as if our wits go out the window as soon as our hopes are raised. I feel that I could have saved myself one abusive relationship and another that was incredibly toxic if I'd done even a little detective work.

Not until I was thirty-six years old did I finally have my lawyer do a business background check—and a friend do a reputational background check—on the man who is now my husband. It was right before I first visited his hometown, which I knew was an important step in our relationship. I felt I was being sneaky, but I had been burned twice before on the verge of getting engaged. He came through with flying colors, and I was able to enjoy the visit with a lot more peace of mind. I was quite embarrassed when he found out about my inquiries, but he respected me more for it!

There's a Reason You Broke Up the First (or Second, or Third) Time

If you're thinking about getting back together with an ex, remember that there's a reason you broke up. Maybe more than one. So ask yourself the single most important question: What has changed? Not who is sorry, or how you feel, but specifically regarding the real issues that caused the breakup. Has your ex changed? Do they have a plan to make amends or behave differently in the future? (If you were to blame, do you have a plan?) If the answer is no, you're in for the same old heartbreak all over again, this time compounded with the painful awareness that you should have known better.

> Two people who broke up can never be friends. If they're friends, they're either still in love or they never were.

Parting Words

To be in a stressful or loveless marriage is one of the most acute forms of suffering there is. In China, we call it *shou ku*, to endure (or eat) bitterness. I'm hoping that some of the suggestions and observations in this chapter might help you learn from the mistakes of others, including mine! I'll leave you with something my husband said to me when we started dating. He had made it very clear from the get-go that he wanted me to be his wife, and one day I said, "You don't know me that well. What if I turn out to be crazy?" He replied, "As a businessman, I've seen every type of human being there is. I can tell that you are a good and kind person. And as long as I'm good to you, you'll be good to me." And it has turned out to be true. He's so kind and supportive and loving that I feel I can't do enough for him. Some happiness is luck, but bringing our best self to our love relationships is within our control.

A Few Words About Weddings

For those who don't want or need to go down the wedding etiquette rabbit hole, here is my cheat sheet (no pun intended).

Wedding Invitations

- Send your wedding invitations at least eight weeks ahead, longer for a destination wedding.
- Set the RSVP deadline for two to three weeks before the wedding.
- Clarify if it's adults only or children are included by stating each guest by name.
- You don't have to give every guest a plus-one if space is tight.
- Couples who are married, engaged, or living together must be invited together.
- Don't use a false start time—wedding ceremonies are the one event people show up for early.
- Including registry information on your invitations or your save-the-dates looks greedy, so put it discreetly on your wedding website.

What to Wear to a Wedding

Although most contemporary weddings are sunset affairs that segue into the evening, they were traditionally daytime ceremonies to which one would wear pastel (soft pinks, yellows, blues). If you're attending a daytime wedding, match the color of your bag with the color of your shoes—nude is safe for summer—and add a fascinator (a hat without a brim that you fasten to your hair) for that je ne sais quoi. Wearing shiny sequins, velvet, or intricate lace is more suited for the evening (save sparkle for when the sun goes down, otherwise it looks tacky!). For evening weddings, the dress code is usually black tie, to which women can wear a dressy cocktail dress or long gown.

No matter the time of day, and generally across cultures, it goes without saying you should not wear all white. All black is frowned upon as well; it is, however, acceptable to wear black and white together, or with another color. And avoid red—the bride will not appreciate you vying for attention.

Comfort is key, especially for weddings that last the whole day (and night) long, so choose your shoes with care . . . nothing is more unattractive than hobbling around with blisters on your feet.

How Not to Be *That* Wedding Guest

- Don't wear white.
- Don't give a toast while tipsy. You're more likely to spill the beans about past indiscretions of the bride or groom.

- Don't sleep with any of the bride's or bridegroom's exes.
- Don't injure someone in an attempt to catch the wedding bouquet. This is not the time to announce you're on the market and hope to be standing where the bride is next year.

Ugly Bridesmaids' Dresses

"Teal, the color of gangrene." That line from *The Wedding Planner* encapsulates the apparent desire of some brides to humiliate their best friends in the quest to keep them in her shadow for the day. Is this any way to reward your besties, who have been by your side through the bloody warfare that is dating in the twenty-first century? In fairness, this desire is probably unconscious, or perhaps just a misguided attempt to match the bridesmaids to an unwise reception color scheme (think periwinkle and seafoam green, coral and turquoise). Just because it's on the tablecloth doesn't mean your poor bridesmaids have to wear it on their backs. Remember, if they are the setting and you are the diamond, you will benefit from their looking beautiful. I've only been a bridesmaid once, for my best friend's, Masha's, wedding, and I recommend her approach. She chose a color and a designer and gave us a choice of two necklines.

Mothers of the bride are expected to be tasteful and discreet, although my friend Lena reported that her normally conservative mother-in-law unaccountably showed up at the reception in a swirly, rainbow-hued psychedelic print dress. Weddings bring out strange behavior in people, most of which they don't understand themselves.

What to Wear to a Bridal Shower

Wear something one notch down from what you would wear to the wedding. Black is a no-no, but choose something you would wear to a fancy luncheon. Find out in advance how casual or formal the event will be, and a good rule for attendees is to wear something like a pantsuit, skirt suit, or high-neck sheath dress. If the event is more casual, however, a blouse and trousers, flowy dress, or jumpsuit are appropriate. And no obvious logo prints, neon colors, or statement jewelry—it's time to look nice, not loud. Stay traditional—with a twist.

Wedding Gifts

In the West, the question of what to give as a wedding gift takes up considerable headspace the moment we receive the invitation. We are not as straightforward as the Chinese, who give red envelopes stuffed with cash at the check-in table before dinner. Depending on your budget and relationship with the couple, you should spend between $50 and $150 for your gift. While there is no maximum, don't go below $50!

1. **Refer to the wedding registry:** Browsing online for wedding gifts is overwhelming and unnecessary if a couple has already set up a wedding registry. This curated wish list will include items they are bound to need and love at a range of prices. Don't spin your wheels when you don't need to, because going off-registry runs the risk of gifting something they already have, don't like, or don't have the space for!

162

2. **Choose something related to their love story:** If they got engaged in Italy, you can gift them a pasta maker. If their first date was walking their dogs together, gift them a set of exquisite handmade pet accessories. Finecomb their social media and wedding website for clues.

3. **Send the gift before the wedding:** Punctuality is important in wedding gift etiquette. The earliest you can send a gift is shortly after receiving the wedding invitation, and at the very latest within three months after the wedding date. (Traditionally it was a year, but things have sped up since then.) Do not bring your gift on the actual day—especially if it's a destination wedding. It might very well get lost amid the chaos and the couple will have a thousand other things that need their attention!

Global tradition says that gifts should go toward the couple's new home. My favorite fail-proof wedding gift is from an exquisite tableware brand, which the couple can use or display in their home. For friends I am less close with, I will go with a beautiful serving platter, or a pair of unique mugs. Silver picture frames are also ideal for commemorating the couple's special moments. And it goes without saying that the items should be beautifully (even professionally) gift wrapped!

Bridal Shower Gifts

Unlike wedding gifts, which should be bought on registry and sent directly to the couple's home, bridal gifts should be off-registry and brought with you to the occasion. This is because opening gifts is a traditional activity at most bridal showers. Yes, you are expected to give a gift for both the wedding and the bridal shower, but the two gifts don't have to be equal in value. The bridal shower gift should be smaller, the rule being at least one-third of what you would spend on the wedding gift.

This is your opportunity to be creative for either just the bride or the couple. Coasters, a ring dish, a cozy throw, a leather-bound journal, a pushpin map for them to track their travels are all thoughtful and fun gifts that won't break the bank.

It is perfectly acceptable if you don't want to separate out the gifts for the bridal shower and wedding and choose instead to give one big-ticket gift, but you must inform the couple. At the minimum, bring a card to the bridal shower with a note that a gift is on the way. If you want to get it over with, send the gift before the shower and mention both events in the card.

Wedding Speeches and Toasts

Traditionally, the father of the bride makes the first speech, although nowadays both of the bride's parents (or even the groom's) may also speak, depending on who is giving the wedding—since they are technically the hosts of the event. If the father of the bride speaks, he should not make jokes about his exhilaration at finally finding someone to take his daughter off his hands, nor should he be so giddy as to say anything that will embarrass the bride and groom. Jokes about how the groom is better (or worse) than exes, or bets on how long they will stay married will not be appreciated. A moving speech should make the audience laugh, cry, and feel inspired.

Next comes the speech by the groom, which almost always goes well. All he has to do is speak from the heart about how happy he is on the joyous day. (The bride traditionally does not speak, although everything is up for grabs nowadays. If you want to, go for it.) It's the speech by the best man that has the highest likelihood of disaster. Often delivered while drunk in homage to the good old days and rarely sparing the gory details, these toasts are meant to be funny but often end up cringeworthy (or worse). The groom should give his best man a stern talking to beforehand about what stays in Vegas and is never mentioned after the bachelor party. Maids of honor sometimes speak as well, so everyone should keep it short. The gaggle of giggling bridesmaids coming to the microphone at once is a new tradition that should not be encouraged.

Especially if you are asked to give a toast as a guest, remember that you are not the star of the show and keep it brief. Go for humor and pathos—people are inclined to laugh and cry at a wedding, so it won't take much to get them there.

DATING AND RELATIONSHIPS: DIGITAL ETIQUETTE

Texting Tips

An outdated rule of the past is don't text first, don't text last, and don't text twice. But if you like someone, show initiative—life is too short to waste playing guessing games. Still, etiquette helps:

- Don't ever just say "hi/ hey/ hello." Follow it up with a purpose—like making plans, especially early on.

- No stream of consciousness texts. Keep them short, fun, and flirtatious. Avoid lengthy messages that provide more chances of being misunderstood—or boring. The same goes for ranting. In fact, if you are in a bad mood or feeling emotional, refrain from texting someone you want to date.

- Just as you would match someone's conversational pace in person, match their response time. You are protecting yourself by not looking overeager. Spelling and grammar matter more than you think—now is not the time to type "how r u 2 day?" And use exclamation points and emojis sparingly.

- Don't text excessively. Sending consecutive texts makes you look clingy and insecure. If the exchange descends into angry demands to know where the other person is and who they are with, it has crossed over into the land of controlling and even abusive behavior. Don't do it. If you're on the receiving end, dump them immediately.

- Don't make big decisions over text, and never jump to conclusions about delayed replies. You don't want to risk overreacting and looking like a psycho. Any initial follow-up should be presented in the spirit of caring, such as "I haven't heard from you all day—are you okay?" When it comes to any issues that need nuance or finesse, know when to pick up the phone and call.

Social Media Boundaries

Have an honest conversation about your social media boundaries early in the relationship. Ask your partner what they do and don't feel comfortable sharing, especially anything related to your relationship. And don't snoop on their phone. Just as with eavesdropping, if do you find something, you won't like what you find—and then you won't be able to bring it up without admitting what you did. Double jeopardy!

It's never too late to show off your new partner on social media. As with announcing a pregnancy, there's no harm in waiting three months or so until the relationship is on solid footing, exclusive, or has official status. It will be embarrassing if you post too soon and then break up, though . . .

At the other end of the spectrum, it's a very personal decision as to whether to follow your ex on social media or like their pictures. There's usually a correlation between how much that ex means to you and whether or not you can follow them on social media. If you feel nothing when you see their posts with their new partner, then go for it.

LOVE: FAQ

Who should pay on the first date?

There is so much confusion about this issue that it clearly reflects a deep-seated societal conflict. In the US, the divide seems to be generational, but even younger people who favor splitting the bill on subsequent dates lean toward having the man pay on the first date. In Asian, Arab, and Latin American cultures, men certainly pay. In Germany, the Nordic countries, and most other places in the world, letting a woman pay on a first date is a sign of disinterest. But once again, it's a generational as well as geographical thing, and norms are changing, albeit slowly.

How do you split costs elegantly?

It's more elegant to alternate who pays than to split bills down the middle, which takes the romance out of it. If you don't pay half of the overall cost of your dates, you might want to pick up some small tabs and give the occasional thoughtful gift to show your appreciation and gratitude.

I always feel it's an awkward dance when I get into a car with my date. Who should get into the car first?

With traditional gender roles, men should let women into the car on the pavement side, and then walk behind the car *to the other door and get in. Do NOT let a woman shuffle across the seat, especially in a skirt and heels.*

What to do when a potential partner shows all the signs that they like you, but says they're just being friendly?

They might have some inner conflict they're trying to resolve, or they could have an existing partner lurking in the background—we don't know. Don't let them toy with your emotions. It's not your job to resolve their problem. If they really want you, they'll sort it out themself.

How soon into dating should we ask about relationship status ("What are we?")?

Depends on you—ask when you need to know if they have the same level of interest to protect yourself before going further.

Is it okay for a woman to chase a man?

Yes, what century is it? A revealing scene in the Netflix documentary Harry & Meghan *is when she says she called him after their first date to say she was only in London for one more day and if he wanted to have dinner the next evening—and look where that led them. But don't force it—if someone doesn't reply to your last two messages, retreat with dignity.*

How to say you're a single mom on the first date?

Play it by ear, but your deadline is the third date.

When and how to introduce the kids?
Only when the relationship becomes somewhat serious. You don't want to scar your children by introducing them to every person you sleep with.

Is there any etiquette for one-night stands?
There is a lot of chatter about this on the internet, but my advice is simple. BEFORE: Make sure it's consensual (which means limiting alcohol as much as humanly possible). DURING: Use protection. AFTER: Protect your self-respect. Don't confuse sex with intimacy, and don't dawdle if it's clearly time to leave. If you've done the deed at your place and you want him to clear out, say your mother is stopping by within the hour.

How does a woman ask a man to get intimate?
Men don't need to be asked. If he doesn't try, he's just not that into you.

How to show and explain to someone how you like to get aroused?
First ask them to show you how they like to get aroused. That way when you share your instructions, it looks reciprocal and not out of left field.

What is the shaving etiquette for pubic hair?
*There's a funny scene in the series **Younger** where a millennial successfully tries to pass for fifteen years younger until she's in the locker room and her twenty-something colleagues spot her (unshaved) pubic hair. "What IS that?" they scream. It's a generational thing. Blame it on porn.*

Is it okay to tell your dinner date to put their cell phone away?

Only if you do it teasingly or flirtatiously, for example saying with a smile, "I want to know what's got your attention more than me!" On the other hand, using a cell phone excessively on a date is a number one deal-breaker, so you're giving them fair warning.

How should you handle your date drinking too much at dinner?

Keep giving them water and call them an Uber. If they're really out of control, see if you can contact one of their friends to get them home safely. Your most important responsibility is to make sure they do not get behind the wheel of a car.

Is there any etiquette for dating a married man?

Aside from don't? Etiquette is not ethics, as I always say, so I won't judge. But other people will. Choose your confidants sparingly. Know your boundaries and expectations and make sure the arrangement is something you can live with. Even if you can, you will spend a lot of time in the shadows. Expect to be lonely on weekends and holidays. An affair is not a real relationship, but of course that's what makes it exciting—for the adulterer, at least. Affairs rarely survive the transition to actual relationships: they lose the excitement that fueled them. PS: If someone leaves their partner for you, don't be surprised if you're next. "When you marry your mistress," as the notorious womanizer Sir James Goldsmith once said, "you create a job vacancy."

How do you break up with someone?

Be direct, decisive, and above all kind. How you break up should be proportional to how serious the relationship was. If it was a fling, you can duck out by saying you're swamped with work. A formal breakup is arrogant if the relationship was casual. But if there were feelings

174

(I say this despite my own behavior!) then the only acceptable way is face-to-face.

How important is it that your family and friends like your prospective partner?

Your family and friends know you well, and if they dislike your prospective partner they probably have good reason. At the same time, you should be the judge of the soundness of their rationale. Is your father a controlling patriarch who thinks that no man is good enough for his daughter? Is your friend jealous of you spending so much time with your partner? If you decide to continue the relationship, at some point you may have to sacrifice one for the other. Make sure you are making the right choice!

I have been dating my boyfriend for four years. I am thirty-four and he is three years older. He tells me that he loves me, but whenever I bring up plans for the future, he gets mad and asks me why I want to "ruin a good thing" by putting a label on it. I'm afraid that if I push him too far, he'll break up with me. What should I do?

The scariest part is not that he put you off but that he doesn't even give you the safe space to discuss your future. Leave.

When is it appropriate to leave some of my things at his place? E.g., toothbrush, underwear, clothes . . .

Where your possessions "live" should feel like a natural outgrowth of the relationship. The fact that you're even asking this question indicates that something is amiss. A friend of mine told me that she spent every weekend at her boyfriend's apartment but felt uncomfortable leaving any of her things there. She finally decided to put a few toiletries under the sink in the bathroom. When she put on her coat to leave that Sunday night, she found her toothbrush, moisturizer, and tampons in a clear plastic sandwich bag by the front door. Message received!

I started seeing someone recently who is very busy with their career. How can I tell them I want to see them more?

If you choose to be with someone who is ambitious, you must be supportive of their career. If you ask someone to make sacrifices for you, no matter what they say in the moment, they could very well hold it against you and resent you later on. Focus on quality of time spent together instead of quantity. You can say, "I really appreciate the time you take out of work to spend with me." Positive reinforcement works best.

How do I help my partner have better table manners without sounding bossy?

There is no good answer to this question. When it's your partner, you have to pick and choose your battles. Save your etiquette for your children.

How do I lovingly tell my spouse that he got some traits from his mother (whom he dislikes)?

You don't. His mother is off limits. Even if he criticizes her, you should tread carefully.

After how long in a relationship can I fart in the presence of my significant other?

The answer is never, if you can help it. Of course we're all human, but as Ralph Waldo Emerson said, "Lovers should guard their strangeness." The standard is no different than you would use for someone you don't know.

Catherine Zeta-Jones said that the secret to a long-lasting marriage was separate bathrooms. Even if that can't literally be true, the idea is sound. You don't want to piss away all the mystery in your relationship.

How should I respond when my partner is controlling?

I'm going to take a hard line on this one based on bitter personal experience: break up with them, fast. That is one big red flag. It's only going to get worse as time goes on. If you're already married, divorce them! There's no way to control a controlling person. Control is often linked to abuse, so don't try to minimize the issue.

What to do when a conversation gets heated? Walk away? Do I say anything?

Don't add fuel to the fire. If you need a time-out, ask for one but agree to come back to each other at a stated time (e.g., in two hours) to show commitment. If you keep your tone slow, calm, and kind throughout, then hopefully it shouldn't get heated!

Should you leave your partner to "feel better" if they had a bad day?

It depends on your partner. Are they the type who needs to blow off steam on their own at the gym? Or can you easily change their mood by entertaining them with lighthearted topics? Do some pilot testing and fine-tune as you go.

My parents are pressing me to meet my boyfriend, but we've only been going out for a few months. Isn't this too soon?

Politely ask them not to put the cart before the horse.

Can we show public displays of intimacy with our partner in front of parents?

It depends on how much PDA your parents show in front of you. If your parents are affectionate, you are permitted some gestures of affection, but keep it brief. Elongated displays make everyone uncomfortable—and are a sign of possessiveness and insecurity rather than affection.

How do you handle exes who come back into your life?

If it was a serious ex and you broke up because of commitment issues, when they come back then it has to be for marriage.

Is there etiquette around regifting something received from a friend?

I'm a big fan of regifting, but there are three rules you must be sure to follow: 1. Ensure that it is brand new and in original packaging. 2. Regift in a separate social circle. 3. Remove any telltale gift card that was addressed to you!

How to uninvite guests that your family invited to your wedding (if you are paying for it)?

Ideally, the misbehaving family members would clean up their own mess, but if they cannot be counted on, then you'll have to do it yourself. Call up the guests—yes, matters of importance and delicacy at least merit a phone call. Sound terribly apologetic and explain that your family extended invitations without your consent and exceeded the maximum capacity of the venue.

Is it appropriate to show our love story via PowerPoint or video?

There has been a recent trend in some countries to show PowerPoint presentations or videos at wedding dinners. They begin by describing the bride and groom's childhood, climaxing with how they met, and ending with the proposal. Sometimes videos can go on and on. Despite the age of digital and an urge to share all, remember that technology should be reserved for the office, and applying it to a wedding is tacky.

How do I seat my divorced parents at my wedding?

Make sure that divorced parents are not sitting at tables too close to one another. Both of your parents will want to sit in places of honor at your wedding reception, but neither should sit at the bridal table. Rather, each parent should host their own table. Giving them space will let them relax and enjoy themselves. If you make the controversial move to not invite a particularly toxic parent, you may be forgiven. It's your day.

Do plus-ones get to be in formal wedding pictures?

Technically, formal wedding pictures should be prioritized for family members. But if it's a multiyear relationship that is basically like (or on its way to) marriage, they should be included. The bride and groom may not want random plus-ones they personally don't know well in their formal wedding pictures. A considerate plus-one should know when to bow out of a formal wedding picture instead of having to be asked.

Is there a good way to politely wind up a text conversation that won't seem to end?

A one-word answer followed by a period or exclamation point is the best way to bring texting to a close (e.g., Got it./Thanks./OK!). If the other person isn't getting the hint, say, "Stepping into a meeting/ Starting some work now, chat later!"

When and how should I suggest our text conversations move "offline"?

The sooner you can steer an online flirtation into a real-life date the better, or you might risk ending up in a textationship! Establish the basics (name, age, job, relationship status, hobbies), and if there is chemistry, make a date. "Do you want to grab a drink?" is the go-to classic. You can also make it a natural extension of your similarities ("Let's walk our dogs together!" or "I love Indian food too. Let's go get some!"). Or make it a seamless transition ("I can tell you more in person").

PART FOUR

FAMILY

One of the oldest human needs is having someone to wonder where you are when you don't come home at night.

—MARGARET MEAD

If the family lives in harmony, all affairs will prosper.

—CHINESE PROVERB

Home is the place where, when you have to go there, they have to take you in.

—ROBERT FROST

Your Best Self with Family

At the bare minimum, those we love deserve to be treated with common courtesy, but we often treat our family members worse than strangers. There's a global stereotype that Americans treat strangers like family and their family like strangers. Obviously, this is an exaggeration, but it gets at an important truth. It's easy to be polite on a superficial level, but behaving well with those we see day in and day out is much more of a challenge.

Our family knows how to push our buttons because they installed them! But we shouldn't assume that we can treat them like dirt just because they're going to love us anyway. Kindness, like charity, should begin at home. This chapter lays down some ground rules for being your best self with those you can't live with, but can't live without.

The Fourth Secret of Social Fluency: Harmony

Interacting with others in a smooth and harmonious way is the fourth secret of social fluency. All roads lead from home, where our self-image—and our habits—are formed. Yet no subject is so fraught as that of family because it is fundamentally tied to our feelings of safety and whether or not we belong in this world. Think of the family as a chamber orchestra: each instrument plays in a different register to produce a beautiful effect. Or cacophony. Everyone has a part to play, and ideally the result is a harmonious whole, but what if families can't even agree on what piece they're playing, let alone who should play what instrument? That's when trouble ensues.

Don't Reserve Your Kindness for Strangers

As I was growing up, my father (in contrast to my unpredictable mother) was almost always even-tempered and civil. His brothers are like that too, polite even when they disagree. My mother's family, on the other hand, is far more informal because they are much closer. They are gossipy, opinionated, and intensely interested in each other's business. Needless to say, spats among them are far more common. Upon reflection, I unwittingly take on the characteristics of each side of the family when I am with them!

My takeaway from these two different styles is focus on respect. You're not always going to like your family or agree with them, nor they with you. But you can strive for tolerance.

The Four Commandments of Courteous Cohabitation

Thou shalt not

I. Leave your jackets, hats, and shoes where they land when you take them off. Neither shall you drop your clothes on the floor.

II. Forget to take out the trash.

III. Leave dishes in the sink or elsewhere around the house.

IV. Be unaware of the noise you are making—music, appliances, video games, loud talking, stomping . . .

Six Keys to a Happy Family

Tolstoy wrote, "Happy families are all alike . . ." That might not be true in every way, but here are six keys that happy families seem to strike more often than unhappy ones:

1. Don't pass each other first thing in the day without saying good morning, or last thing in the evening without saying good night.
It's not just civilized to acknowledge the existence of another human being, it's basic humanity.

2. Limit arguments to three minutes.
In years of research, John Gottman, one of the world's foremost relationship experts, has observed that the most important points in any argument are made in the first three minutes. After that, people say the same things over and over again—louder.

3. Discuss money openly.
Money is a hot-button issue for most families. Couples don't want to talk about it, and parents don't want to talk about it with their children. The earlier the subject is raised in a relationship, the better. It's important to know whether you are financially compatible before getting married, and discussing money decisions openly is one component of a healthy relationship.

Carrying that openness over into the parent-child relationship is vital, but most parents these days would rather brave the sex discussion than talk about money with their kids. That's too bad because parents are the biggest influence on their children's financial behavior. Studies have shown that most of the habits people will use to manage their money are set by the age of seven! But it's never too late. Having frank discussions about what you can and can't afford in terms of allowance, schooling, vacations, and housing will make you closer as a family. Don't procrastinate.

4. Never let anyone eat alone.

Family meals might not be possible in our crazy, overscheduled world, but making it a rule that nobody in the family eats alone will greatly contribute to mental and physical health. That means no phones or reading at the table.

5. Don't judge yourself by your intentions, and don't judge your family by their actions.

We like to think of ourselves as rational, but many of our decisions are made unconsciously based on mental shortcuts. Called cognitive biases, these shortcuts are as instantaneous as physical reflexes. The problem is that what we gain in speed, we lose in accuracy.

There are literally dozens of cognitive biases, but the one that causes the most trouble in family relationships is *correspondence bias*. When someone else makes a mistake, we tend to assume they are doing it because that is "how they are"—e.g., "You haven't done much today because you're lazy." When we err ourselves, we often attribute the cause to situational factors—e.g., "I didn't get anything done today because people kept distracting me." When we suffer from correspondence bias, we chalk up other people's behavior to their personal disposition while letting ourselves off the hook because of external factors. We also fail to give others credit for variability, leading to those damning accusations of "you always" do this or that.

Blaming other people and avoiding personal recrimination can become a vicious cycle in a family, but you can break it by using empathy: putting yourself in the place of the other person. What this will look like in real life is a two-step process. You can't stop your automatic internal attribution ("She didn't buy milk because she's selfish") but you can follow it with a more measured consideration of whether an external attribution is more accurate ("Maybe she was in a hurry and didn't have time").

6. Bite your tongue.

It has been said that anger is a condition in which the tongue works faster than the mind, and anyone who has blurted out a criticism they regret a moment later will bear witness to that. Sometimes we wish we had an "unsend" button on our cheek. But anger is also a subtle foe. In the heat of the moment, we may feel that we are incredibly eloquent, but we fail to see the long-term ramifications, the devastation that will result from our flow of angry eloquence. A secret of family happiness, as a friend always says, is "Zip the lip." Get into the habit of pausing before speaking. And refrain from correcting an error if the error doesn't hurt anyone.

> "If you speak when angry, you'll make the best speech you'll ever regret."
>
> —GROUCHO MARX

The comedian Craig Ferguson said it took him three marriages to learn that there are three things you must always ask yourself before you say anything:

- Does this need to be said?
- Does this need to be said by me?
- Does this need to be said by me now?

If the information is unimportant, such as a case of fake news or a harmless embellishment of the truth, it is probably not worth correcting. But even if your correction passes the "three questions" test, don't just drop the bomb of your correct information. Even the most evolved person will get defensive about being exposed as wrong.

Say someone is about to act on incorrect information in a way that will be harmful to them or others, including you. First ask them how they reached their conclusion, then give options about alternatives. "Really? Where did you read that eating vegetables is unhealthier than eating meat? Are there other studies that came to different conclusions?" Stay curious and open. If they still won't budge, lead with empathy when you deliver the bombshell of your correction. It's not about being right, it's about doing the right thing—and preserving their ego is part of that.

Boundary Basics

Do not

1. Open a closed door without knocking—and waiting to hear "Come in."
2. Take each other's belongings without asking—that includes money!
3. Spill each other's secrets.
4. Embarrass your relatives in front of their friends.
5. Make arrangements for others without getting permission in advance.
6. Read each other's email or text messages.

Respect Personal Boundaries

There are physical boundaries and emotional boundaries, and sometimes it's hard to tell them apart. It certainly *feels* emotional when someone transgresses a physical boundary, and people who can't respect one type generally don't respect the other.

For siblings living together, it's a matter of territory: Who gets more? In an economy of scarcity, whether of material possessions or of love, these battles can become vicious. Between parents and children, it's about autonomy. Teenagers need to assert they can act on their own, which incurs the famous pitched battles we have all observed—and even fought ourselves—in the past.

I know I had some epic battles with my very strict mother, who would barge into my room, usually around six a.m., even if she knew I had been out late the night before. She would sit on the edge of the bed and start talking *at* me. "Why are you so lazy? You should come hiking with me and your father. We've already played squash and had breakfast." (This was during summer vacation weekends.)

Once you are a young adult, parents should have gotten the message that you have your own life, and the parameters of intimacy should be established. Ah, that word "should." If things were as they should be, I wouldn't be writing this book!

One problem is that adulthood is coming later and later, and the demarcation is not as clear as it used to be. In previous generations, children moved out after college and established their own lives and that was that. These days, they often can't afford to do that right away and sometimes still accept financial help from their parents. So they're still treating their parents' home as if it were their childhood home, which makes their parents treat them like children.

A common theme I hear is that parents feel they have the right to invade their adult children's living space and treat it as an extension of their own. They use their children's homes as a sort of free motel if there is a nearby airport or wedding, for example, or invite themselves for extended visits, whether or not there are grandchildren. Even if they do ask, it's hard to say no.

Parents have always found it hard to accept their children's independence, but these fuzzy boundaries make it even harder for them to let go. It requires constant vigilance not to backslide into old habits. Sometimes the violated boundary is not physical but involves a barrage of texts or voice messages. A nonparent who acted like that would be accused of stalking! And indeed, it is a similar violation of boundaries not to respect the fact that the other person has not replied—either because they can't, or because they choose not to.

So what is the etiquette of redrawing a boundary without turning it into a rift? To draw a new boundary you must first be clear about it in your own mind. Think about what you actually want—not just about how irritated you are about being invaded or disrespected. And don't act out or make a statement based on the specific situation that pushed you over the edge. For example, don't threaten in that moment to put a deadbolt on your door so they can't barge in, or threaten to block them on your phone. This is no time for grand gestures. Take a step back and consider what the real issue is. Then craft a response that will get you what you want in the long term while preserving good relations.

How to Defang Nosy Relatives

Just as little children are taught to keep their hands to themselves, adults must be taught to keep their opinions to themselves. Like all courses of instruction, this can be a slow and laborious process, but it is possible. You can get your relatives to stay out of your relationship with your partner, for example, if you respond with humor and confidence, but you must have a plan. My cousin Gerran, for example, brilliantly handled our family demanding grandkids before he was ready. When he and his wife finally grew tired of being pestered, he announced, "We don't want to have kids." That silenced everyone—for a while. Then he switched it up by saying, "We'll have kids when Sara gets married." My rejoinder to that was, "Well, then you'll never have kids because I'm never getting married!" Double whammy! My poor grandmother—her oldest grandson refused to have kids, and her oldest granddaughter refused to get married! The family was joyfully surprised a few years later when they had an adorable baby boy—and my grandmother's happiness was complete when I got married shortly thereafter. But we did it in our own time.

When I married my husband and began spending time in his hometown, there was a lot of overt and covert speculation among his friends and relatives as to when I would get pregnant. "Don't delay," his friends would hint to me. When I gained noticeable weight from feasting over the Chinese New Year, my mother-in-law repeatedly asked my husband if I was pregnant. Every time someone asks me to my face, I reply with a smile and say softly, "Yes, I need to work hard toward this goal." What else can they say to that? Try harder?!

Nosy relatives are a fact of life and a mainstay of holiday celebrations. There is no way to prevent questions about when you're going to get a job, or a better job if you have one, or when you're going to meet someone, and if you're seeing someone, when you're getting married, and if you're married when you're having children, and if you have children . . . It never ends, so get used to it. Make it a game to come up with a strategy beforehand. Or you can use my favorite technique: etiquette jujitsu. When someone asks an intrusive question, agree with them (in principle): "You're right! It would be wonderful if we had children." Then quickly change the topic to something juicy enough that they won't notice (maybe why your cousin isn't married yet). Agreeing takes the wind out of their sails; take advantage of the moment of confusion before they trim them and start in on you again.

How to Be a Fairy Stepmother

Which is more hated, a stepmother or a mother-in-law? Hard to say, but being a stepmother is certainly one of the most challenging and thankless roles in the world. One-third of Americans are involved in a blended family in some capacity, so this is a subject many of us have experience with from one side or the other—or both. So here are a few words of advice for stepmothers or stepmothers-to-be:

1. **Know your place.** You're not their mother, and you never will be. So don't even try.
2. **Let the kids take the lead.** When you first meet the children, particularly if they're young, keep it low-key and neutral. You're just a friend of their father's/

mother's. Things will go better if you make them think they had a hand in choosing you!

3. **Be a cool "auntie," not a disciplinarian.** Until you gain their trust, you're in no position to do anything but be a source of fun and pleasure. Hand out treats, let them bend the rules, make a fuss over them. When respect has been established (years) down the road, you might have the standing to start enforcing rules.

4. **Read the parenting plan and talk about money—before you get married.** All the details of your new life—including how much of your partner's resources will be available after alimony and child support—should be spelled out in black and white. Don't be embarrassed to ask, especially if you're thinking of having children together. This is your future, and you owe it to both of you (and to the children) to know whether it's something you can handle.

5. **Don't forget to focus on your primary relationship.** It's easy to lose sight of why you signed up for all this in the first place. Make time for just the two of you—no discussion of children, exes, etc.—for at least one evening a week. And don't forget to keep having sex!

6. **Be patient.** The closeness will develop over time if you are prudent and loving—and bite your tongue. As the children get older, it will be you whom they consult for the tricky life issues that they'd prefer not to share with their parents.

I come from a blended family myself, as my father remarried not long after my mother died when I was twenty-one. My step-mother has never tried to be my mother; she is more of a friendly acquaintance. And she has always been careful to give me my own time with Dad on my visits home. I appreciate her tact and like her all the more for it.

What Do Children Owe Their Parents?

All this talk about boundaries raises the important question of what parents and adult children actually owe each other. What parents owe children is the simpler half of the equation. Most boomer parents believe they should pay for their children's needs through college, but the responsibility ends there. Gen X and millennial parents are more likely to believe they should continue to help their children beyond graduation—with a deposit for a home, for example. But the question is really just one of degree: of how much, and for how long?

What—and whether—children owe their aging parents is a far more profound subject. In the East, people are very upfront about saying you have children to look after you in your old age. In the West, on the other hand, people are concerned about not being a burden on their children. Far from dragging their feet, some Americans who can afford it are proactively moving into retirement communities that provide graduated levels of care depending on their state of health. A lot of this, however, depends on financial circumstances. Care is expensive so it needs to be planned for, just like buying a house or paying for an education.

If you were lovingly raised, regardless of culture, you will feel good about taking care of an aging parent, although the responsibility might weigh heavily on you, and they might bridle at their increasing dependence on you. It will seem that you have come full circle; there will be a rightness about it. The trouble arises when there is a discrepancy between what is being asked and what you are willing to give.

Is there still an obligation to help in those cases where someone was abused or neglected in childhood, or simply had very little contact with their parent while growing up? The philosopher and *New York Times* ethics columnist Kwame Anthony Appiah asserts, "Children don't have obligations to their parents merely by virtue of being biologically related. Those obligations arise only from a proper relationship with them." In his view, you might still make a decision to be helpful, but there is not an absolute obligation.

It is at this point that Eastern culture diverges sharply from the West. In most Asian societies, blood translates automatically into responsibility. Traditional Chinese culture is based on filial piety, and even to this day it is not uncommon for young Chinese adults to start giving their parents 10 percent of their salary as soon as they graduate from college. Chinese parents will sacrifice everything for their child's success, which is why they demand so much in return.

Neither culture is right or wrong; there are strong arguments to be made for both sides. One thing is for sure—no matter how we have been mistreated as children (short of actual abuse), when we see our parents age and suffer, we will feel guilty for not helping them. We should keep in mind that no matter how bad our relationship with our parents, when they die we will miss them.

Only Lend as Much as You're Willing to Lose

So many family feuds are about money, where greed and mistrust poison any good feelings that might have existed. There's no way I can resolve inheritance disputes here, but what I can say is that when family members ask for money, only lend as much as you're willing to lose. I wish I had listened when my dad tried to teach me that. When I was much younger, a distant relative asked my dad for money, and he gave her a small loan and said she didn't need to return it. That way, he said, if she pays me back, I'll be pleasantly surprised. If she doesn't—and it was clear to me he thought that was much more likely—there are no hard feelings. Good advice.

> "Family quarrels are bitter things. They don't go according to any rules. They're not like aches or wounds, they're more like splits in the skin that won't heal because there's not enough material."
>
> —F. SCOTT FITZGERALD

If you want to draw a boundary with a relative to whom you have given money in the past, try not to switch off the tap abruptly. Sit down with them first and do a budget. Help them come up with a plan for the future. And if this is the *final* time you intend to help them before they can get back on their feet, draw up a promissory note charging a small amount of interest and ask them to sign it. That makes it official, gives them incentive to pay you back, and enables you to claim the unpaid debt on your taxes in the unfortunate event that they don't make good.

How to Handle Sibling Rivalry

The second oldest story in the Bible—after the creation of Adam and Eve—is Cain murdering his brother, Abel, because he thought God played favorites. No matter what your opinion regarding the Bible, you have to appreciate the dark humor: the instant God created siblings, they were at each other's throats. From the standpoint of evolutionary biology, it makes sense. Siblings are vying for limited resources. And in an economy of scarcity—where there isn't enough money or love to go around—the battles can become fierce.

My friend Elizabeth is similar in age to her younger sister, Kelly. They are both high-powered, strong-willed, and successful. One day, Kelly called from Japan and asked Elizabeth if she was interested in a blue light therapy device to treat and prevent acne. She could get a deal if she bought three, and she was thinking of keeping one and sending one to their mother and one to Elizabeth—if she would use it. Although Elizabeth didn't care one way or the other, she agreed, and her sister had the device delivered to her office. A few months later, Elizabeth visited her mother, who asked if she'd tried the device. Elizabeth had misplaced it, so her mother lent her hers until she could locate it. Another few months went by until the three of them were all together at dinner and their mother casually asked Elizabeth if she ever found the acne device. Kelly snapped on that like a shark on fresh meat. "Wait, you lost what I gave you? Why didn't you tell me? What if the delivery person had stolen it?" Elizabeth got angry in return. "It's just an inanimate object. So if you give it to me, it's a gift to me. It's none of your business what happens to it after that, even if I lose it. You were the one who really wanted to get it. You're morally blackmailing me." Kelly started to cry. "You never appreciate my gifts! I'm never giving you another thing!" Elizabeth said, "Why are you overreacting? Tell me how much it cost and I'll just give you the money." Kelly might have been overemotional, but Elizabeth really knew how to rub salt into the wound.

There will always be times when we have a different point of view from someone we care about. Here is my favorite tool for difficult conversations. It is a simplified version of the ladder of inference, a mental model introduced in 1970 by Chris Argyris. By breaking down the steps we take to reach conclusions from a simple piece of data, the model gives us the opportunity to correct misperceptions along the way.

Kelly's point of view:
1. Facts: I gifted you a $1,500 skincare device. I had it specially delivered, but you don't even know where it is anymore.
2. My interpretation POV: if you don't care about things I gift you, you don't care about ME.
3. How it made me feel: unimportant, uncared for, unloved.
4. Ask: What was your POV? What happened in your interpretation?

Elizabeth's point of view:
1. Facts: you had it delivered to my office at a time when I was navigating a conflict with my boss and changing jobs.
2. My interpretation POV: an object is an object and you are overreacting; I only said yes to be agreeable.

197

3. How it made me feel: emotionally blackmailed, manipulated, angry.
4. Repeat with Kelly's POV to continue the process of reconciliation.

There is a Chinese proverb that says, "The soft can subdue the hard," so use softness to defuse tensions rather than worsening them.

One important thing: There are two sides to every story, but that doesn't mean that responsibility (okay, blame) is always apportioned fifty-fifty. Sometimes the fault is more the other person's than yours, but you still have to clean up your side of the street.

Playing Favorites

No matter how hard your parents try, they will always play favorites. You're sure your mother prefers your sister, or your brother, although she insists, "I love all my children the same." Nonsense. And—ahem—why would she have to keep repeating it unless someone (you?) was trying to get her to say otherwise? Parents are human. So what if they do prefer your brother or sister to you? Don't try to get them to confess to having a favorite. Would it really make you feel better to hear the words you've always dreaded coming out of your mother's mouth? Of course not. Be a grown-up.

My friend Grace often complains to me that her little sister, Alice, is her parents' favorite. Alice has always been clingy and kittenish with them, and she would sit on their father's lap until the age of fourteen, which Grace felt was very inappropriate. During high school, Alice spent a lot of time with her parents while Grace was out drinking and partying with friends. And recently Alice—now a corporate lawyer—has been giving more money to her parents than Grace, who founded a start-up and has less disposable income. Grace, like many Taiwanese children, feels it's her duty to give 10 percent of her salary to her parents because they supported her throughout her life until her education was complete. (An exception is Taiwanese Christians, who give 5 to 10 percent to the church instead.)

Because of COVID, Grace didn't see her parents for three years, citing work pressures and travel restrictions, while her sister visited them multiple times. This only cemented the existing favoritism. Up until college, the parents insisted the sisters hug and kiss at the end of every fight. But now that their parents are older, they don't even tell them to stop fighting, which bothers Grace even more. The hard truth that Grace will have to accept is that you can't change anyone else, even—or especially—your parents.

Raising Children Who Will Change the World

As the child of a Tiger Mom, I was often told that the ends justify the means, and that all the pain was worth it because of how well I turned out. That belief was thrown into question a few years ago at an education conference in London. After I gave my short talk, the coordinator—a rather nondescript, bossy person in her seventies—complimented me and gave me her business card. She told me to look her up if I ever came to San Francisco.

I glanced at the name—Esther Wojcicki. The surname looked vaguely familiar, but I couldn't remember where I'd seen it before. During the break, when everybody was comparing notes, someone said, "Oh, you know who I met today? The mother of Anne and Susan Wojcicki!" I said, "Wait—the CEOs of 23andMe and YouTube Anne and Susan?" He replied, "Yeah, she's raised two of the richest women in the world and the third one is some brilliant researcher." That was the woman who had given me her card.

Six months later I did get to San Francisco. I emailed Esther, and she told me to come over to the high school in Palo Alto where she teaches journalism. We spent the afternoon hanging out on the grass with her students. She was so amazing, I had to ask her, "Esther, what are your tips to raising such successful children, because all of my students who are mothers in China will want to know." She laughed and started telling me about a debate she'd had with Amy Chua, who wrote *Battle Hymn of the Tiger Mom*. During the debate, which was organized by the Mexican conference La Cuidad de las Ideas, Amy insisted on going first and exceeded her time limits—in true Tiger Mom style. The important thing, though, was that when they were talking about raising a child, all Amy could talk about was how unpleasant and difficult it was, and how annoying that children didn't listen to you and that you had to force them to do things. Esther talked about the joy of raising children, and how it was a discovery process and an adventure. She and her husband, now a retired physics professor, always encouraged their children to explore further and made sure that learning was fun.

If you look at the results, which is what being a Tiger Mom is ostensibly all about, one of Amy's children went into the military, which in Asian culture is a huge no-no; the other is covered with tattoos, tantamount in Asian culture to saying a parent has failed, since it's the ultimate form of rebellion. Esther's relaxed style has been dubbed "Panda Parenting," in honor of that animal's notoriously lazy habits. But she doesn't consider the approach lazy. She says Panda Moms "give children scaffolding to let them go free. Instead of always intervening, you only help when they need it." In any case, she adds, "your control over your child is over by the time they're fourteen."

I wish I could say Tiger mothering was on the way out in China. It is, but it's been replaced by something even more extreme: jiwa or "chicken" parenting. The term refers to an antiquated quack treatment of injecting someone with fresh chicken blood to stimulate energy. The academic stakes are so high that parents are willing to do almost anything to ensure their children's success. In public school in China, from primary school on to college, every one of your test results is posted on a wall along with your name and ranking. It's very much part of Asian shaming culture. The pressure is unbearable. Not long ago, it was in the news that a child ran away because he came in fourth out of a hundred in his class and was verbally abused by his parents. He couldn't take it anymore. The story went viral in China because there was a sense that we have to stop parenting like this.

But it's always been so, at least as far as I can remember. You're never good enough. If you get a 99, they want to know where the other 1 percent is. The expectations keep you from getting an inflated ego, but they also damage your self-confidence and make for really unhappy parents and unhappy kids. It occurs to me now for the first time that I was raised by a Tiger Mom and a Panda Dad. When I struggled initially at Exeter, my dad's advice was, "Aim for an A to be your 'normal state of affairs,' and getting straight As will be normal!" I printed this out and stuck it on my wall along with all the other inspirational quotes from him. And funnily enough, within months I was getting straight As!

It was certainly a point scored for the Panda Moms when Sasha, an eleven-year-old French boy in my apartment compound, spontaneously sat down and started playing the piano during one of our pandemic lockdown parties. There were about sixty people there, eating and drinking and merrymaking, when suddenly this masterful music floated across the room. Everyone fell quiet—it was literally concert pianist level. He had no sheet music, and when his performance came to an end all the Chinese mothers flocked to his parents and said, "How do you do it? How do you make him play so well?" His parents blushed and replied, "We don't make him do anything. It's something he enjoys." The Chinese mothers walked away looking incredulous and a little baffled.

I happened to be standing next to my downstairs neighbors, so to be polite I said, "Your son's playing is coming along nicely." I could hear him every night, at eight o'clock on the dot, playing the same song. Plink plink. "Oh," they said, embarrassed. "You can hear him? We close the windows before he starts to play!" Esther Wojcicki, by the way, is on the record for letting her daughters quit their music lessons!

Mind Your Children's Manners

Somewhere along the line, it feels like people have picked up the idea that manners are bad for children because they impose limits. That's what manners are for! We are not born civilized, and many of us do not behave in a civilized way even as adults. But we can at least instruct our children to behave less like the little savages they naturally are.

It's one thing to tolerate such behavior within the home, but it's another to inflict it on the world at large. And what is cute in a three-year-old is less so in a thirteen-year-old, and positively frightening at thirty. Take Kaiser Wilhelm II, grandson to Queen Victoria and the man who began World War I, who stabbed someone in the foot with his sword when he was a toddler. I stopped seeing a good friend because I simply could not tolerate the unbridled shrieking of her child and the way she catered to and enabled that behavior. I know he wasn't raised by wolves because my friend is a lovely person, but he certainly acted that way. (And no, there was nothing the matter with him, and she had plenty of help.)

The worst thing for a misbehaving child is an oblivious parent. You can try hinting, "She seems like she's a handful to manage," but chances are the parent will miss the cue. All you can do is put away breakable objects and/or have one area specifically for the kids, if that's possible. When inviting, I say, "We're having an adults-only gathering." If you're the host, you set the rules. People either come or don't come. It's their choice.

Remember, if your child breaks something, you should insist on replacing it. Even if your host refuses, which they probably will, you should do it anyway and have the replacement sent to their home.

Nine Steps to Raising Socially Fluent Children

Across cultures, our children are a reflection of ourselves. If our child is not capable of giving another human being the most basic of greetings, then we're doing something wrong. Social fluency begins early, with teaching children these simple steps:

1. Say please and thank you.
2. Look adults in the eye and greet them.
3. Address adults as Mr. and Mrs. (unless the adult instructs you otherwise).
4. Use a napkin, not your sleeve.
5. Hold your fork and knife correctly.
6. Chew with your mouth closed.
7. Never open a door without knocking first.
8. Don't stare or point.
9. Always cover your mouth when you cough or sneeze.

Beyond these steps, how do you bring up a well-mannered child? I got to see the process in action when I attended a family dinner at my grandmother's house. I don't go back to Hong Kong very often, so a lot of my cousins were there, including my cousin Gerran, his wife Winnie, and their two-year-old son Lucas.

In Chinese culture, you train children to greet each adult individually. Lucas (who was in the middle of eating a cookie) was unwilling to say, "Hi, Auntie Sara." That was unusual since he is adorable and so well-mannered that he is practically like a mini adult. Winnie, who is a model of motherly patience, said, "Say hi to Auntie Sara. She's just returned from a trip." When he turned his head away and refused, she repeated her request in a calm voice and patient manner. After this happened about five more times, Winnie gently removed the cookie from his hand. He glared at her but did not give in. Winnie tried again. "Lucas, every time there's an adult at the table you have to greet them. Otherwise I'm not going to let you have your cookie." He continued to ignore me.

At about the ten-minute mark, I started to feel really uncomfortable and said, "Winnie, it's all right. You can let it go." But she was resolute. "Lucas, you have to learn good manners and say hi to Auntie Sara. She's over there. She's come back from a trip. Just say hi." The battle of wills continued until about minute twenty-three when I heard a small voice from across the room. "Hi, Auntie Sara." Lucas got his cookie back. And that, ladies and gentlemen, is how you raise a child.

> A parent can give a child no greater gift than beautiful manners.

Parenting is about patience and persistence, whether kids are four or fourteen. When they're angling for a later bedtime or a bigger allowance, they'll keep asking—once, twice, three times. Often parents will give up in annoyance, thinking it's too much trouble and a waste of time to keep holding out. But to cave in is to encourage bad behavior. Constantly saying yes to a child is not love. It's laziness.

After the encounter with Lucas and the cookie, I reflected on how I had inadvertently undercut Winnie's discipline by saying it was no big deal whether Lucas said hello to me. It reminded me of a story my Georgetown psychology professor, Steven Sabat, shared with the class about how his daughter was rude to her grandparents at dinner, putting her feet up on the table and refusing to put her phone away. When he told her that her behavior was inexcusable and sent her to her room, her grandparents protested, "Oh no, it's all right. Don't be harsh with her. We don't mind." He felt the need to discipline his parents before turning back to his daughter and repeating his order that she go to her room.

> Remember, never interfere with the primary disciplinarian no matter who you are—and that includes undercutting the other parent! One of the most frequent causes of divorce is opposing parenting styles.

The issue of grandparents spoiling children is a big one these days. Some grandparents consider it a God-given right, even a duty to spoil their grandchildren, but it's called "spoiling" for a reason. It can ruin months, even years of careful discipline. And it can be a very passive-aggressive move. My friend Tiffany told me that when her five-year-old son visited her parents for a long weekend, they bought him a forbidden video game player and let him eat marshmallow fluff from the jar even though sugar was not allowed in her home. Worse, they did this with a certain glee. You can try speaking with recalcitrant grandparents, but in the end, as with difficult parent figures in a custody arrangement, visits might have to be supervised.

In-laws and Outlaws

Maybe we hate our mother-in-law because we are expected to. Or maybe she dislikes us first. We are engaged in a perpetual tug-of-war over who loves her son more, or whom he loves more. No one will ever be good enough for him, unless she is too good for him, in which case who does that uppity interloper think she is, anyway?

Ugh. What's a daughter-in-law to do? Read on. As Madame Néri, who ran the Swiss finishing school I attended, used to say, "It's better to learn from us than from your mother-in-law."

Before I begin, it's only fair to admit that sometimes the fault lies with us. I was speaking with my friend Melanie when she was dating her now husband, and she was complaining that her future in-laws were not easy to deal with. "What do they have to complain about?" I asked. "You're a huge catch." It was the truth. After a little digging, I discovered that she had regifted them a huge leg of Ibérico ham and neglected to remove the card that was addressed to her. Bad move, especially so early in the relationship. She compounded looking dishonest (by regifting and pretending it was new) with looking disrespectful (by being too careless to remove the gift card). Double whammy.

> The one form of humor common to all cultures is the mother-in-law joke.

Other times, the fault has nothing to do with us. One potential mother-in-law successfully sabotaged my relationship with her son (and, in retrospect, she did me a favor).

Things with Matthew's mother started off well. In the beginning, she would buy me gifts, prepare my favorite foods, and welcome me on their family holidays. But then our relationship started to sour. Every time I entered their house I felt like I was stepping into a den of snakes. Nothing I could do was right; no gift I gave was good enough. Matthew reprimanded me for everything. The gourmet food basket was considered "too corporate." The exquisite Italian handmade hairbrush was deemed "too personal." When I complimented her cooking on a specific dish, she gave me a withering look and said, "Oh I didn't cook that. It's takeout." I never let my shock at her rudeness show, but consistently kept a smile on my face no matter how she bullied me. Since I could never seem to say the right thing, I eventually decided the best solution was to follow his sister's example and stay silent. Then Matthew berated me for "not trying hard enough." He said it was *my* responsibility to make an effort with his parents.

In relationships, it is a partner's responsibility to handle their own family. It will tell you a lot about your future relationship with someone if you see whether they do or don't try to finesse any difficulties that arise. Are they loyal to you? Do they try to mend fences? And if it is a man, the relationship he has with his mother will shed a lot of light on how he views women in general and you in particular. (Matthew had a toxic relationship with his mother.)

So what are the takeaways?

1. The key to harmony with your mother-in-law is to be close but not too close. A girlfriend of mine who manages her mother-in-law very well recommended the Chinese saying "maintain soup bowl distance" between you, meaning sufficiently close that a bowl of hot soup will not get cold when it's carried between the two houses. Too far and relations are chilly; too close and you risk oversharing. Your primary goal is to protect your marriage. You don't want to be sitting there having tea with your mother-in-law and finding yourself confiding in her. My friend Susanna says she got lured into sharing her marital troubles, which her mother-in-law promptly reported to her

son, who was justifiably outraged. He might not be your husband one day, but he will never stop being her son. It was a clever way of sabotaging the relationship, and she regrets having fallen for it. Don't be fooled. (On the other hand, if you have a daughter-in-law you hate, perhaps you should use this tool!)

2. If there is any conflict or confrontation, let your husband handle it. His family is his responsibility, just as your family is yours. As a test fairly early in the relationship, set up or observe a situation where there is a choice between you and his mother and see whom he chooses. Heed the results. If your husband doesn't choose you, you're in for a world of trouble down the line.

3. Take heart: although your mother-in-law might have the upper hand in the beginning, the power dynamic will flip if grandchildren are produced. After all, you will control access, whereupon an uneasy détente can be established.

How to Win Over Your Mother-In-Law

You might not literally have to learn a different language to speak to your mother-in-law like I did, but it's a good metaphor. As if our own families weren't challenging enough, when we marry into another, we are expected to decode an entirely new microculture without—here's the rub—understanding the context that gave rise to them. It's an enormous challenge. Try too hard and you're bound to make errors. Hang back and you'll likely be accused of being standoffish. And of course there's always the class issue, although many Americans pretend it doesn't exist and hate to discuss it. Someone is almost always marrying "up" or "down."

When it was finally sinking in that my boyfriend would become my husband, I decided to learn his dialect. China is home to 1.4 billion people, over 90 percent of whom speak a dialect; there are over a thousand distinct dialects. My husband's hometown is located a four-hour drive from Shanghai, in Zhejiang province. In his city of Lishui alone, with a population of 2.5 million, there are a dozen dialects. Towns only three hundred feet apart have dialects that sound as dissimilar as German and French.

"When someone asked me how to be rude to his mother-in-law without getting caught, I replied that the only way to do that is by being extremely polite."

—JUDITH MARTIN

It became apparent that our life together in China would consist of us living between Shanghai and Lishui. And in Lishui, just as in any city around the world, the locals like to speak their local dialect among each other. Which meant that to entertain and engage with me, they would speak Mandarin (the official language of China), but when they spoke among each other, they would revert to the Lishui dialect. The Lishui dialect sounds completely different from Cantonese, the dialect my family speaks, and Mandarin, which I learned in school.

One day, I called my husband and asked him to find a local tutor to teach me the Lishui dialect. "There's absolutely no need," he replied. "Just spend more time in Lishui and listen to me and my friends talk." Now, as somebody who has grown up learning many different languages, I know that is not the way to learn effectively. In addition to "language immersion" you need to understand basic vocabulary and grammar so you know how to string a sentence together.

Coincidentally, Tina, one of my former assistants, was from Lishui. She introduced me to her primary school friend who worked in the prosecutor's office and who insisted on teaching me without charge on her lunch break. In two weeks, I began replying to my husband's friends in dialect. They were visibly impressed. Then I began speaking to my mother-in-law in her native dialect. She was delighted.

I didn't have to show fluency. I prioritized learning practical phrases that would please them such as "This food is delicious," "I arrived in Lishui yesterday," and "I wish you good health." Now when I have tea alone with my mother-in-law and I catch the meaning of something she says, I use the "FBI trick" of mirroring back the last few words. "My neighbor was hanging her laundry all the way into my garden today, she is so annoying." "So annoying," I say, nodding vigorously. My mother-in-law will beam. "You see? I know you understand exactly what I'm talking about!" My husband gets such a kick out of this. Whether it's language or other cultural lessons, what's important is the intent and the effort to slide seamlessly into my husband's world as though I always belonged.

What Do You Do If Your In-Law Violates Your Boundaries?

Sometimes an in-law's bad behavior is borderline or open to interpretation, but sometimes it is just plain out of line. Soon after my friend Evelyn moved in with the man she would later marry (and divorce!), she and her future mother-in-law went shoe shopping. That charming lady took the opportunity to share, out of nowhere, "You know, if you were to break up with my son, I have no doubt he would have no trouble finding someone as good as you, or even better." Luckily, Evelyn was looking down at a pair of boots at the time so her expression was unreadable. When she got home, she shared this story with her future husband, who looked increasingly outraged as she spoke. He immediately picked up the phone, but instead of making a call, he drew his arm back as if to throw it. Then he set it carefully back on the table without dialing. "Don't you ever bring this up again," he said.

In the unfortunate event that something like this happens to you, sit your partner down, calmly relate the facts, be firm about your own boundaries, and wait to see if your partner treats you like a partner. Remember, even though you might be boiling with rage, don't say something about their parent you could later regret (they certainly will never forget). Think about how you would feel if they insulted your parents.

If your partner doesn't immediately come to your defense, give them the benefit of the doubt. They could be in fear or denial, and you should be the judge of that. Try to guide them to stand up to their parent ("Would you be comfortable next time you are alone to ask her to leave these decisions to me?"). If your partner, like Evelyn's, still doesn't stand up for and with you—or even worse, belittles you—take this as a big red flag.

Family Feuds

Do you know what the word *resentment* literally means? To feel again. And again and again and again. That gnawing pain when you keep replaying the same scene in your mind, trying out different endings in an attempt to lessen the anger and the hurt. Good luck. That's why the best approach to resentments is to prevent them from forming in the first place if humanly possible. You'll be saving yourself a world of hurt.

The most painful conflicts are family conflicts. We can feel betrayed beyond measure when what is supposed to be our source of support, love, and encouragement becomes a source of pain. The battle between the desire to cut off contact and the elemental need to stay in touch is exhausting. I have a friend whose sister has always had a troubled relationship with her parents, especially her mother. She enrolled in a weeklong intensive healing workshop in the countryside (no cell phones!) famous for helping people accept and overcome past emotional trauma. Then, instead of reconciling with her parents, she cut them off completely. That was eight years ago, and it is not an uncommon story.

> "Before you embark on a journey of revenge, dig two graves."
>
> —CONFUCIUS

More people than ever are "divorcing" their parents, for a variety of reasons ranging from actual abuse or neglect in childhood to a difference in values. The problem with cutting your parents out of your life is that the incision doesn't heal. Relationships don't exist just in the real world: they exist in our minds. How many times have you replayed an argument with someone who wasn't there? Estrangements are open wounds with no chance of repair. Sometimes they are the best solution, but they should only be entered into as an absolute last resort.

So what is the "etiquette" of dealing with toxic family members that we can't cut out of our lives? I'll share a painful story from my own past to illustrate. At the end of my senior year of college, my mother was diagnosed with terminal liver cancer. I flew home to Hong Kong to see her, and we spent a week together. I was prepared to miss my exams and graduate a year late, but my mother was adamant that I return to school and finish on time. "You have worked so hard for this," she said, "and you have such an amazing job lined up in New York. I won't allow you to jeopardize that. If you want to make me happy, you'll go back now." My mother knew I loved her, and I knew she was telling the truth. We both knew, too, although we never said it out loud, that our relationship was always better long distance. When I was in boarding school, we spoke every night on the phone for an hour, but when I came home we tended to butt heads. For us, it wasn't about the quantity of time we spent face-to-face but the quality of the relationship. Sadly, she died three months later.

I came to find out that my mother's younger siblings in San Francisco went around during those months telling everyone in the family who would listen that I was "unfilial" while my mother was dying. They believed, in traditional Chinese fashion, that I should have dropped everything to stay by her bedside into perpetuity. But they had no idea what my relationship was with my mother, and they certainly had no right to be poisoning family relations behind my back. My solution? I didn't see them for ten years.

I finally did relent and visit my aunt and uncle because I was in town on a business trip and my beloved grandmother was staying with them. I saw them for only half a day, during which I maintained a distant gaze and a pleasant smile. The last straw, though, was when they tried a few months later to prevent me from seeing my own grandmother. They lied and told me, "Stay away from Grandma because it stresses her out to see you," and

I believed them! That's the problem with family feuds: the collateral damage. Months later my cousin Adrianne, from my dad's side of the family, set me straight and insisted, "She's getting old. You have to reach out to her." Of course, my grandmother was overjoyed to hear from me and expressed confusion and pain at my silence.

Beware of hurting others who are not directly in the line of fire. I eventually blocked my aunt and uncle on my phone because I decided I no longer want to have toxic people in my life even if they are related to me, but it took me five more years to do this. I did not come to this decision lightly.

It can be tempting to cut ties with difficult relatives, thinking, "Someday they'll die and this problem will go away." There's just one catch: relationships don't end with death. You can carry on that feud and relive that old argument for the rest of your life, regardless of whether the person is still alive or not. You won't be magically freed when they're no longer walking the face of the earth. Don't fool yourself. So while you have the chance, if only for your own peace of mind, use every opportunity to mend fences.

> Family feuds are often about money, but not always about the lack of it. Sometimes having money just gives families more to fight about.

Don't Fight a "Cold War": Dealing with Silent Treatments

Sometimes when we are angry, we don't respond to others because of a mature desire not to lash out. At other times, we are so overwhelmed by our emotions that we literally can't speak.

This is called diffuse physiological arousal (DPA), or emotional flooding, and while it can look like the silent treatment, it's actually a form of self-preservation. In contrast, the real silent treatment is a deliberate attempt to punish someone close for having hurt us. In its extreme form, it can be a type of abuse.

My friend Alana, who lives with her parents, had a trivial conflict with her mother a couple years ago. Her mother overreacted and, feeling disrespected, didn't speak to her for two weeks. Alana would ask her a question; her mother would pretend she didn't exist. Alana apologized and pleaded with her to acknowledge her in some way. Nothing. Feeling erased, Alana became seriously depressed. Her father wisely suggested family therapy not only for the three of them but for the other siblings as well. Clearly this was not his first rodeo with the silent treatment. Happily, it helped, and they all go in for maintenance every month.

I'm all too familiar with the silent treatment since my mother was prone to it too. She would sulk and carry her sour attitude for days. This is the script I wish I'd been able to use back then, to be delivered in person or in writing:

I'm sorry for [insert offense here]. It really hurts me that you're not speaking to me. It's counterproductive, and it hurts both of us. I understand that you're not ready to speak to me now and I respect that, but as time goes by it becomes more difficult rather than less to make peace. I'm ready to speak with you anytime to see how we can work through this. So I'll check back in with you later [today/this week].

Flip side: If you have a tendency to fight a cold war and ignore someone, you should tell them, "I'm not in a place where I can speak to you right now. I need some time, and I'll let you know when I'm ready."

What to Do When a Relative Goes Down the Political Rabbit Hole

There's a lot of discussion about the "radicalization of youth" on social media, but many of my friends have had more experience with the radicalization of the elderly! I can't tell you how many times I have heard about formerly lovely relatives being transformed into monsters of intolerance and bigotry by social media's manipulative recommendation algorithms. Not that any of us is immune, but older people are easy marks for the "alternative influence network," as much as their parents may have been for phone scammers. This radicalization, for that is not too strong a word, is a worldwide phenomenon. Many of my friends say with a pained smile that their parents "go to WhatsApp University," a disparaging term for being brainwashed by fake news.

This trend is incredibly frightening and also sad, because it's tearing families apart. So what do you do when your parent or another close relative develops extreme political views that make you uncomfortable? You can try asking them to stop discussing politics with you, but the problem is that they often insist on bringing up the subject in every conversation. That is a feature of radicalization: they want to convert you too. If that doesn't work, you can try a little speech:

I respect where you're coming from and why you have these views, but I feel like your political views have become so extreme that we can't even have a two-way dialogue anymore. I feel I'm not being listened to. And any criticism of xyz you take as a personal affront. You feel I'm criticizing you as a person, which isn't true. I see your side, I'm just trying to stay objective here. I feel that every conversation we have goes back to why xyz is bad/evil and you launch into a political tirade.

This will only have a chance of succeeding if your delivery is soft and loving. If it doesn't work (and you can't hack into their computer and change their feeds to something more wholesome—just kidding), the last resort is to make clear exactly how alienating your relative's behavior is. Ask them if they value their opinions more than they value your relationship. Or just tell them in a calm and straightforward way, "I do not want to discuss politics." Repeat if they continue or change the topic or leave the room if they won't stop. Sometimes stating that you won't engage and then following through is the best tactic.

FAMILY: DIGITAL ETIQUETTE

Texting

Texting is the primary means of communication among most families, spearheaded by younger people's dislike of email and phone-calling for everyday communication. Eventually, the older generation realized that their emails and voicemails were going unanswered and got with the program. When parents and other elders start texting, however, miscommunications can ensue. Why? Punctuation is the main culprit. So here is a primer on punctuation for the textually challenged. Give this to someone who needs it!

A Primer on Punctuation

Language and punctuation are different online than they are IRL, and it's important for older users to understand that they don't speak the language as fluently as their younger counterparts. People who privilege face-to-face interaction and formal speech miss nuances of digital communication and often miscommunicate in ways they aren't even aware of. For example, Gen X and boomers often use ellipses, which make millennials and Gen Z (or younger) break out in hives . . . Older people should avoid them out of courtesy. Keep in mind that if millennials or Gen Z use punctuation in their texts it means they're either mad at you or about to give you horrible news.

Just as a traveler to a foreign country should take pains to learn the local customs, those who did not grow up on social media should understand that they are the visitors. Your grasp of the local customs should go beyond knowing not to use ALL CAPS. On the other hand, every generation should make allowances for the others' texting styles. Keeping in mind the age of the person sending the message will avoid much misunderstanding on the part of the recipient. K? K.

Family Chats

Most family chats are essentially group chats composed entirely of memes that no one reads. The upside is that no one's feelings get hurt because no one reads them.

Social Media

Social media has become generationally bifurcated. If Gen Z and younger millennials have Facebook at all, it's to keep in touch with their parents—or grandparents. Young people are always moving on to the next platform, just as they know it's time to stop using slang when their parents pick it up. Generational overlap will always be limited, as it should be.

FAMILY: FAQ

I moved back home recently after living on my own since college. Even though I'm twenty-five, my parents just barge into my room as if I were a child. How do I set ground rules/boundaries around my personal space?

It's hard to blame your parents for reverting to old habits. The last time they saw you, you were a dependent. Now you're a young adult. Here's a question, though: Are you paying rent or contributing to the household in any meaningful way? (And I don't mean grudgingly clearing the table or doing your own laundry and no one else's.) If you're still behaving like a child, you can't blame them for treating you like one. So before you ask for ground rules to be redrawn, think about how the adult you differs from the old you. Then your request for privacy and respect will be on solid footing.

What should you do if your parents continue to talk with their mouths full?

Try to ignore it. It's too late to raise them properly! Luckily you learned manners, even if you had to pick them up somewhere else.

My dad calls me until I pick up and will leave me ten missed calls. How do I deal with it?

The thing about this obsessive behavior is that it's equivalent to a panic attack. Anyone who behaves this way—parent or not—is having some sort of existential crisis. To them, it feels like you have just died—until they hear your voice when you pick up the phone. This kind of behavior indicates a psychological issue for which your parent should receive help. If they don't want to go to therapy, a last resort might be offering to go to family therapy, at least for a few sessions, to get them started.

My family keeps asking me whether I'm dating anyone. This makes me really uncomfortable because I haven't found anyone yet. How do I respond?

Why does this make you feel uncomfortable? Don't be embarrassed about having standards or waiting for the right person. Be confident and tell them as much! "I haven't found someone I want to be with yet, but I'll let you know when I do." Don't forget to smile when you say it.

How should I respond when my family asks about my salary?

If your family is financially subsidizing your lifestyle, they deserve to know. But if they're not, and you're financially independent, you don't have to tell anyone (except maybe your partner). Unfortunately not all parents will agree, so if you don't want to share, use humor to deflect—"Don't worry, Dad. I'm a big girl now!" Don't make this a big issue by confronting them head-on because that will offend them. FYI—it's always smarter to be underestimated.

My family overstays their welcome at my house. How do I kick them out?

Set the boundary while you still have the upper hand—before they arrive. "We would love to have you stay with us! But pest control is coming on March 8th so we'll need to clear the house by then—one week should be enough, right?"

How do I exit the family business without hard feelings?

Nothing creates more family conflict than discord in a family business. If you were driven to make this decision, it means that there are already hard feelings. Your only hope now is to exit the family business without exiting the family. Go to the key decision-maker and work out a plan **together** *before presenting it to the other members. If you don't appear to build consensus, they will feel blindsided.*

How do I bring up inheritance?

You don't, at least not directly. The question is insensitive on a number of levels. It is a wise thing to have a discussion with your parents about leaving instructions for what they want you to do in the event that they become ill (health care proxy, living will, etc.) or die (funeral arrangements, whether they have made a will). But the contents of the will are their business unless they choose to share them with you. People are living longer and are often lucky not to outlive their money, let alone have any left over to give their children. If they fed, clothed, and educated you, be grateful. Hanging on the expectation of an inheritance is entitled, unwise, and unseemly.

How to handle relatives or other people criticizing my child-rearing?

Just like when you receive any other criticism, first look within. Don't let yourself be that hated parent who can find no wrong with their own child. Nobody in the world is a perfect parent so be grateful for early cues that could save you from rearing a monster. If, after conducting a split-second internal 360 review, you feel your relatives are out of line, bite your tongue and change the subject. Refuse to give energy to their criticisms, and they will roll off of you.

How to push back respectfully when my in-laws are spoiling my children?

Apply the principle of "Put your foot down and get someone else to do the dirty work." In other words, get your husband/wife to tell them they won't be able to see your kids anymore if they persist. Don't take the heat yourself. They had their chance to raise children as they saw fit. No do-overs.

How do I refuse food from pushy relatives without offending?

In many cultures, feeding is a sign of love, so tread carefully—especially if the relative is a homemaker who derives particular pleasure from feeding family members. I personally gain quite a few pounds after a visit to my mother-in-law, who looks at me despondently if I don't finish everything in front of me. Say you are recovering from food poisoning and eat very slowly—so that there are always multiple items on your plate. An empty plate only asks for more servings.

How do I gracefully handle a relative moving in with my family?

If you can handle it, make sure to lay out some "house rules," which you can make seem less targeted by saying they are for "everyone" to follow, and in the spirit of consensus, let "everyone" participate in making them. Before they move in, you should discuss with your partner whether this is a short- or long-term arrangement.

How can I strengthen my relationship when my mother-in-law is adamant about sabotaging it?

Assuming you entered the relationship with eyes wide open, then that is the suffering you chose. At the end of the day, it is up to your partner to make clear to their mother that they put you first. If your partner doesn't respect you, your mother-in-law never will. It is possible your mother-in-law did a bait and switch, in which case you're still screwed.

Am I expected to maintain a relationship with my ex in-laws/ex's family?

Only maintain a relationship with the in-laws if you have children. Act pleasant and never badmouth your ex in front of them. If you don't have children, the universe has not given you a reason to stay connected. Drop the in-laws along with the ex.

How do I handle the uncle who insists on conspiracy theories about everything—just ignore?

We all have someone like this in the family! At best, nod sympathetically but don't reply—any sort of response will likely encourage a rant. If you just can't stand it anymore, humor him to see how far he will go. I like to play dumb and say, "Oh my gosh, I can't believe the government is mandating vaccines purely to get everyone's data! How shocking!"

My dad sends me tedious stuff to read. How do I politely indicate my extreme disinterest?

The best defense is to ignore. Any reply, positive or negative, will only encourage.

PART FIVE

FOOD AND TRAVEL

*As your conscience might trouble you if you do anything
immoral, your sense of embarrassment should
be activated if you do anything unmannerly.*

—JUDITH MARTIN

*Travel makes one modest. You see what a tiny
place you occupy in the world.*

—GUSTAVE FLAUBERT

Your Best Self at the Table—at Home and Away

Now that restaurants have become the primary form of entertainment for many of us, it's more obvious than ever that the basis of social life is sharing food. Anthropologists believe that sharing and dividing food is what sets us apart from other animals. Fulfilling our biological need to eat gave rise to kinship systems, or family ties—along with language, technology, and morality. It also gave rise to much of what we call manners, and the special importance of table manners in the development of civilization cannot be overstated. "Behind every rule of table etiquette," writes anthropologist Margaret Visser, "lurks the determination of each person present to be a diner, not a dish. It is one of the chief roles of etiquette to keep the lid on the violence which the meal being eaten presupposes." We humans might differ from other animals in many ways, but not in terms of our appetite and the lengths to which we will go, in the absence of guardrails, to satisfy it. And when traveling to another country, we are metaphorically guests at another person's table, so similar rules apply.

The Fifth Secret of Social Fluency: Consideration

The fifth and final secret of social fluency is showing consideration—respect for the feelings and rights of others coupled with a desire not to offend. Consideration is a state of heightened awareness. Watching someone talk with their mouth full, we lose our appetite when the point of being at the table is, after all, to share food. Consideration is equally important when traveling to another country, where we are, in effect, guests.

They might do things differently there, but at their table, their rules apply. Our hosts' behavior follows a code—not a microculture this time, but an entire culture—that will remain hidden to us unless we move to their country. That's all the more reason to try not to give offense.

FOOD

Table Manners

"Tell me what you eat and I'll tell you who you are." A famous gourmet wrote that, but as an etiquette instructor who has spent hundreds of hours teaching table manners, I'd amend it to, "Tell me *how* you eat and I'll tell you who you are." Nothing in our public behavior is more revealing than how we convey our food to our mouths. Perhaps unjustly, people make judgments when they watch us eat—about our background and upbringing, and about our delicacy as human beings. Rules for eating vary from culture to culture and evolve over time. It used to be acceptable, for example, to eat spaghetti with your hands, but even that was governed by its own etiquette. In nineteenth-century Naples, you had to lift the strands with your right hand, throw back your head, and drop them skillfully into your open mouth. (And no slurping!)

In previous decades, people learned by watching their elders at the table, but with the disappearance of communal meals and the rise of solitary eating (often in front of some sort of screen), table manners are in abrupt decline. It's quite stunning the number of people I've come across who are well educated and well traveled but have horrendous table manners. That's fine if you're alone, but if you want to make a good impression on a date, a higher up at a business meal, or your future in-laws, it's a very good idea to perfect your table manners. So, let's take it from the (table)top.

First Things First

How to not look like you were raised by wolves

- Put your napkin in your lap when you sit down.
- Don't hold your fork like a shovel.
- Don't hold your knife like a pen.
- Don't reach over others at the table.
- Don't chew with your mouth open or talk with your mouth full.
- Don't lick your knife.
- Don't wolf down your food.

Restaurant 101

Restaurants have become the new theater—meaning it's partly people-watching—for a generation who would often rather spend their disposable income on dining out than on other leisure activities.

Since we do much of our public eating in restaurants, I have decided to give you a very brief course in Restaurant 101. Read through it and commit its main points to memory, and I guarantee you will not commit a single faux pas at a restaurant (or at a private dining table, for that matter) henceforth.

Act One: Making your entrance

Before we even get to the reservation desk, let's stop off at the coatroom. If you are carrying a bunch of shopping bags and an umbrella, or you have a heavy coat, spring for the few dollars and check them. You want to bring as little as possible to the table. If the restaurant doesn't have a coat check, obviously you have no choice. If you're lugging something really bulky, however, you might ask the reservation desk if they can keep an eye on it for you. I've done that when I'm going straight to the airport and have luggage—they understand.

Some people assume it's polite to allow your guest(s) to walk into the restaurant ahead of you, but that's not actually the case. Whoever made the reservation goes first because they are the host. If you're a woman on a date with a man, and he made the reservation, he goes first because he needs to immediately communicate with the maître d' about your reservation.

When the restaurant staff shows you to the table, the host should pause and let guests go first in order to direct them where to sit.

The guest always gets the best seat, which can be a view of the room or of a beautiful sunset or the ocean. The worst view is of a wall, so the host should take that. Sometimes the maître d' will pause behind the chair he or she expects you to take and even pull it out for you, so look for signals. If your host doesn't know the rule and hesitates or seems confused, take the best seat for yourself. If you're the host, remember that people want to be told what to do, so don't say, "Oh, sit anywhere," unless there is a huge group and that makes sense.

Act Two: Settling in and ordering

Now that you've been seated, your first question might be, "Where do I put my bag?" If there's a spare chair, you can put your bag there; if not, put it behind you, between the small of your back and the chair. In very fancy restaurants, you can ask for a bag stool. If the bag is a small clutch, put it on your lap and lay your napkin over it. Never put your purse on the table! Not even if it's a tiny evening bag. If it's a big tote or briefcase, you can put it on the floor under your chair. Don't hang your shoulder bag over the back of the chair. That's not only a really easy way to get your wallet stolen, but it will also be knocked every time someone walks behind you.

Next, napkins. Put your napkin on your lap when your host does. If it's been a minute and they haven't, you can go ahead and do it anyway. If you drop your napkin just pick it up (the five-second rule applies).

> **Pro Tip:** Always keep the napkin folded in half on your lap with the fold open toward you. When you wipe your mouth it's on the inside of the napkin, and when you put it back on your lap it looks from the outside like a clean napkin!

Let's talk about menus. I have a pet peeve about this. While it's true that you look too rushed if you immediately open up your menu, a lot of times people will start talking and completely ignore the menu. I'm generally hungry when I show up for a meal! You should definitely have that first minute or two to chat, but then after that, if it's very clear that nobody is making any moves to open the menu, I like to say, "Oh gosh, we have so much to catch up on. Let's order first. Then we have all the time in the world to talk." Another trick of mine is to say, "So I've heard that the roast chicken here is simply divine," while opening the menu—it's so seamless your dining partner won't even notice.

Sometimes the server will come over and ask if you want to order drinks, and that's fine if people still haven't made up their minds about what they want to order to eat. But I find it amusing when the server tries to make you feel uncomfortable for ordering your drinks and your meal at the same time. It's totally a matter of personal preference whether you order your drinks at the same time as the meal or not. It depends on how long you want to linger at the table. In a fine dining restaurant, you may order wine with the meal, but they still often try to get you to order an aperitif, a cocktail meant to stimulate the appetite. Restaurants make all their money on the booze, not the food. Remember that.

If people seem undecided, I ask them what they're thinking of ordering. Then it turns into a conversation, which seems to speed the process along. When you've decided, you should close your menu as a sign to the server that you're ready to order.

Badass power move I learned from world-famous chef Jean-Georges Vongerichten: When I playfully asked the chef what billionaire founder of Alibaba, Jack Ma, ordered at his restaurant, Jean-Georges replied, "He doesn't really specify what he wants to eat. He says, 'Just put a menu together. Four courses. I have two hours.'" So recently when I treated some family friends to lunch, I tried it out. I handed the menu back to the waiter and said casually, "Three courses. We have one and a half hours." My guests tried to disguise their admiration, but I saw it! Obviously, you should share any dietary restrictions with the server. This only works at restaurants where the chef considers himself an artist; don't try it at a casual or mid-level restaurant. It would be embarrassing if it fell flat!

Act Three: Knives out

Look down at the cutlery in front of you. The basic rule is that you go from the outside in. On the left-hand side are forks, and on the right-hand side are knives and spoons. Let me use an old-fashioned but memorable analogy: if there is an even number, they are couples and should be used together. Every fork that's placed on the left-hand side of the plate is like a wife. She "needs" a right-hand side husband. If there is any additional cutlery that is not paired, you will always find it on the right-hand side. It is considered single and should be used first. The number-one rule is, *Once you pick up your cutlery, it can never touch the table again.* That includes its handle, not just the "dirty bits," so don't lean your knife blade on the plate while the handle rests on the table. I call this being "neither here nor there."

Now for my favorite part of the meal, the bread basket. I confess that I'm a buttervore and eat my butter with a side of bread rather than vice versa. I feel about butter the way Colette did about truffles ("If I can't have too many truffles, I'll do without truffles"). Although I judge a restaurant by its butter, I promise I'm not a snob. Even those little foil-wrapped butter pats floating in a saucer of ice water can be delicious. When they're hard as ice, it's an excuse to eat them whole, as if they were little chocolates.

Now that I've got that out of my system: You should pass the bread basket to others before partaking yourself. Take only one piece of bread from the basket at a time. Break the bread in half over your side plate, and from that half, tear bite-size pieces. Don't put the bread in your palm but hold it in your fingers, close to the plate. Tear off one small piece at a time and butter as you go. If you have a butter knife, use it. You'll find it on or near your side plate. (The size of cutlery usually matches the size of the food it's meant for.) Never put butter on your bread straight from the communal butter dish. Instead, you should put it on your own side plate first. If you have your own solo butter dish, it's okay to use it straight from there.

Put the butter knife completely on the side plate, not leaning partly on the plate and partly on the table. Remember, once you use your butter knife, as with all cutlery, it can never touch the table again. Not even a tiny bit of it.

If there's olive oil and balsamic vinegar on the table, Mediterranean style, you should pour four parts olive oil first followed by one part vinegar on your side dish. (This ratio can be altered depending on your taste.) Break off the bread one small piece at a time before dipping. If there is only one small dish of oil and vinegar for the table, do NOT double-dip unless you know the person you're eating with well enough to share bodily fluids, because that's essentially what you'd be doing! If there are multiple people, choose your moment and use your bread as a sponge, greedily soaking up as much as you can on that first dip. I like to ask the server for individual dishes of oil and vinegar (or butter, as the case may be!). Be considerate, but free.

Act Four: The main event

Once your meal arrives, don't cut all your food into bite-size pieces at once. A surprising number of men seem to do this, in my experience. Perhaps it's a carryover from childhood.

As a rule, you should only start eating when your host picks up their cutlery. If they are preoccupied and haven't started eating, you as a guest should make a show of looking right and left as if to say, "Oh everyone has their food. It's time to dig in." And if the host is oblivious, then just start. NB: It is not permissible in a fancy restaurant to rotate your plate while trying to access a certain food.

Top Ten Rules of Chopstick Etiquette

Do not
1. Play with your chopsticks, just as you would not play with your knife and fork.
2. Stab or pierce food with chopsticks.
3. Hover over a dish with your chopsticks, or rummage around looking for the best bits.

---

4. Leave chopsticks standing vertically in a bowl of rice (or other food). This resembles the incense sticks that are offered to dead ancestors.
5. Tap chopsticks on the edge of your bowl. It is a sign of begging.
6. Chew or suck your chopsticks, or let them rest in your mouth.
7. Point with your chopsticks—this is very rude.
8. Pass food from one pair of chopsticks to another. Put the food down on a plate or bowl first.
9. Use just one chopstick.
10. Overlap or cross your chopsticks.

You should stay seated during the meal, so use the restroom before the meal starts or wait until after the main course has been cleared and just before dessert is served. When you want to leave the table for a restroom break, it's elegant to say, "I'm going to wash my hands." Even a simple "Excuse me for a moment" will do. If you're part of a large group, you don't need to announce your departure (more disruptive than simply leaving). Remember, *if you've removed your knife and fork from the table, they can never touch the table again, so rest them on your plate.* Leave your napkin on your seat to signal, *Save my seat, I'm coming back!* (In a nice restaurant, the server will sometimes refold your napkin and put it back on the table, so don't be surprised if you don't find it on your chair when you come back.)

Troubleshooting: If your dish has not come out at the same time as everyone else's, you should tell everyone to please start eating while their food is hot. If someone else's dish has not come out of the kitchen, make a show of caring: "Where's your food? We should ask the server to check up on it." That person should tell everyone to begin, but if they don't, try offering to share some of your dish with them. That ought to work! Again, it's mostly for show. When all else fails, tell them you haven't eaten today and ask if they mind if you dig in!

Which leads us to another thorny question: how to call the server. In Hong Kong and the rest of Asia, you just raise your hand nice and tall, as if you want to be called on in class, and then wiggle your fingers. You don't even have to make eye contact and some-one appears right away. I remember doing this at dinner in a fairly nice restaurant in DC with my friend Jordan from New York. Jordan actually hissed at me, "That's not the way you call the waiter. That's so rude!" "So how do *you* call the waiter?" I asked. It took him at least five minutes to make eye contact with the waiter, and when he finally came over to the table, Jordan was so apologetic he was practically whispering, "I'm so sorry, sir. But could my friend possibly have some hot water?" It was as if he was afraid of offending the man by asking him to do his job. That's the opposite end of the spectrum, of course, but there is a happy medium.

I recommend holding up your hand at ear level to catch their attention and then trying to make eye contact. If they refuse to meet your eye or are dashing around elsewhere, ask the busboy to find them or possibly the manager if they are nearby. There is no need to apologize for asking for service. Ask for good service and tip generously.

I will wrap up with a funny story. I met a friend of mine on a frigid December day in New York for dinner. The place she chose was closed, so we went across the street to see if they had any room. It was Friday night, and the place was packed. As she recounts the story, she told the hostess, "We don't have a reservation," at the same moment I held up two fingers and said, "Table for two." The hostess seated us in the heated outdoor enclosure, which was actually our preference because of the pandemic. The first table was right by the entrance and extremely cold, so I asked to be moved. The waitstaff obliged. The second table, however, was next to a boisterous group and really noisy, so a few minutes later, I asked to be moved to a quieter table. Once again, the waitstaff seemed happy to accommodate us. By then, my friend was looking a little bewildered. "Why are they being so nice?" she asked. I wasn't sure exactly what she meant, but by then I realized it was still too noisy for us to talk, so I asked if they could move us outside and please bring some extra heaters. My friend was now shaking her head. "They gave us a table in a packed restaurant without a reservation and then moved us three times without complaining, all the while keeping your cup refilled with plain hot water. I don't understand how you did it." She still laughs about it, but all I can think is that if you are polite (rather than apologetic) and have an expectation of good service, you will get it.

Act Five: Closing out
When the meal is over and it's time for the check, ask for it if you're the host (whether date, business, or friend) so that the

server knows to give it directly to you. That spares the inevitable awkward wrangling if you intend to pay it yourself. (If you really anticipate a tug-of-war and want to avoid it, you can pay secretly on your way to the restroom.) If the check just appears at the table, be decisive and make it obvious that you're taking care of the bill. If you expect others to split it with you, pause a moment. Your guests should offer promptly to contribute their fair share. If you're a guest, don't hesitate to offer when this moment arrives.

When it's time to leave, place your napkin, clearly used and lightly folded (not crumpled), to the right of your plate. Just as a memory aid: the napkin goes from the *left* of your plate at the beginning of the meal to the *chair* when you take a restroom break to the *right* side of your plate when you leave.

Attending a Dinner Party

At a restaurant, you are only expected to eat, but as a guest at a dinner party, you have a role to play. For hosts wondering how to make up their guest list, the famous food writer M.F.K. Fisher advised, "A good combination would be one married couple, for warm composure; one less firmly established, to add a note of investigation to the talk; and two strangers of either sex, upon whom the better-acquainted diners could sharpen their questioning wits." You get the idea. A dinner party is a performance. And your part begins even before you get there.

RSVP promptly and share any dietary restrictions if your host doesn't ask first. Arrive a few minutes past the appointed time, never late and certainly never early, even if you are "in the neighborhood." Ask what you can bring if you know the person well. Otherwise, bring a bottle of wine (or two, if you are part of a couple) plus, to set yourself apart, a little something extra your host can use at the party or that will look good photographed on social media. You might bring cocktail nibbles to snack on before dinner, or exquisite chocolates for after dessert. Alternatively, a beautifully wrapped condiment like truffle oil will always be welcome. As with so many things, there are cultural differences: in Germany, you give the host a book and the hostess flowers; in France, it's bad manners to give wine; in China, you can never go wrong with bringing specialty foods like fruits. If you bring flowers, make sure they are already in a pot or a vase, and if you want them to be exhibited on the table, make sure the arrangement is low. You can't go wrong with something beautiful your host can either use or eat.

Once you're seated, hold up your end of the conversation. Be witty. Be charming. Talk equally to those seated near you, not only to those you know or find interesting. I try to make it a game to find boring people interesting, or to make humorless people laugh. At the very least, it entertains me.

When the meal begins, if it's family style, always pass dishes to the right. You need not serve people on your left or right if they are peers, unless you want to come across as a really selfless person. If they are elderly or children, you should serve them first and yourself second (or hold the dish and let them serve themselves, if they prefer). The host always serves others first and themself last. Pace yourself as you start eating. You don't want to be noticeably faster or slower than the rest of the table. Take your cue from the host about when to start eating and make sure you're not the slowpoke holding everyone else up. (The host should be the first to start eating and should pace themself with the slowest person.)

GOOD GUEST	BAD GUEST
RSVP promptly and don't back out unless there's a real emergency	Call and ask your host who's coming before committing
Let the host know if you have any dietary restrictions	RSVP late or not at all
	RSVP yes and don't show up
Respect the dress code, but add a little sparkle	Arrive late, drunk, and with an unexpected entourage
Bring at least one bottle of wine, even if you are abstaining yourself	Or worse, arrive early
	Wear workout clothes to show how little you care
Also bring a little something extra, like nibbles to be served with drinks, champagne, or a hostess gift	Bring a cheap bottle of wine or nothing at all
	If you're a couple, bring one bottle max
Arrive a few minutes after the appointed time	Don't tell the host about dietary restrictions and then loudly announce there's nothing here you can eat
Be charming and liven up the party when you can	
Or be altruistic and help out your host with serving, pouring, etc.	Keep your phone on the table at all times and check it constantly during the meal
Always toast the host and compliment the chef (unless the food is so bad that silence is kinder)	Start an argument at dinner or at least raise a highly divisive topic
	Turn on the TV to watch the game
Don't leave without saying goodbye to the host	Bang on the bathroom door and rattle the handle
Be sure to thank the host the next day, whether the party was good or not	Overstay your welcome
	Say and do absolutely nothing the next day

244

Thinking about good guests and bad guests reminds me of a recent experience I had that managed to cram a few rude behaviors into one evening. To belatedly celebrate a friend's birthday, I hosted a small dinner in the private room of an upscale restaurant and told her to bring a friend.

When I host dinners, I usually show up at least twenty minutes early to check the table and plan the menu. But before I had even gotten dressed, about an hour and a half before the appointed dinner time, I received a text message from Alice: "Tom and I came to the restaurant early. Do you mind if we go ahead and order a bottle of wine?" I replied, "Of course, pick any bottle you want! I will rush over right now as well!" I was, however, extremely flustered. It is bad manners to be late, but absolutely worse to be early! And to be so early and completely take over a hostess's reservation is something that wasn't even on my radar, especially since I had made it clear that I would pay the bill.

Alice later explained that they arrived early in order to catch up on their own first. But what would have been better etiquette was to go to a bar next door, and then show up at dinner together.

Communicating dietary restrictions

I am often asked if it is rude to decline foods you don't like at a dinner party. The answer is that your host should ask you in advance if there is anything you can't eat or if you have dietary restrictions. If they don't, and if you have severe restrictions like celiac, veganism, or keeping kosher, you should notify your host soon after you accept the invitation (not the day of, when the menu is already planned). If you have not done so, or if something appears to which you have a strong aversion, take a small portion or quietly skip the offending dish and eat everything else.

Most importantly, do *not* think you're being polite by denying you have restrictions when you do. I had such an experience when I invited an American expat who had been living in China for more than twenty years to my house for dinner. It was to be a casual meal to help her with some research she was conducting, and I asked her in advance if there was anything she didn't eat. She said no, so I planned to serve homemade dumplings. As we sat at the table, I noticed she was breaking apart the dumplings and only eating the meat. "I'm sorry," she said, when she noticed me looking at her questioningly, "but I have celiac." I said, "But I asked you if there was anything you couldn't eat and you said there wasn't." "I know," she said apologetically, "but I didn't want to make a fuss and cause you inconvenience." But she did cause an inconvenience—the serious stress of having nothing else to feed her, which undermined my care as a host.

So don't "spare" your host. You're not doing either of you any favors by withholding information. And if you're on a diet and can't eat anything at all? For myself, I'd answer that by saying, stay home. Nothing puts more of a damper on a dinner party than a guest who doesn't eat.

With any luck, the evening will achieve that wonderful alchemy of intimacy and excitement that only a dinner party can provide. Saying thank you is a must—so what's the best way? I like how the French do it, which is to wait until the next day, because it shows you're still thinking about it.

Throwing a Dinner Party

What about when it's your turn? Propriety suggests reciprocity, or so the Chinese proverb says. If you've been invited to someone's home for dinner more than once, you might decide to bite the bullet and have them over (meanwhile crossing off some other social obligations as well).

The prospect of throwing a dinner party is daunting for many reasons. For starters (no pun intended), it is very revealing to invite someone into your home. As I say in my show, "To know a fish go to the water; to know a bird's song go to the mountains. To know someone you should go to his or her home." We can control the details of our public persona much more carefully than we can our living situation. It's possible to put forward a sophisticated face with the right clothes and a carefully curated social media image, but these are essentially a facade. It's where we live that will tell all, and often much more than we intend. I was friends with a young woman in college who was a well-known socialite (you would recognize her name!). She was always photoshoot ready—impeccably dressed with perfect hair—but when I visited her apartment I was stunned to find it was an absolute pigsty. It communicated that she is someone who is focused on image to the exclusion of all else: the ultimate embodiment of style over substance.

> "The only occasion when the traditions of courtesy permit a hostess to help herself before a woman guest is when she has reason to believe the food is poisoned."
>
> —EMILY POST

The reason it's worth taking the risk of inviting someone into your home is that it can foster instant intimacy in ways that eating in a restaurant never could. And here is where I reassure you: very little of the success of a dinner party has to do with the actual food. It has to do with warmth and a sense of ease, and that begins with the attitude of the host. Your guests will feel comfortable if you are. It all comes down to preparation.

Here are my foolproof rules for how to throw a (relatively) stress-free dinner party:

- Ask guests in advance about dietary restrictions. Sometimes figuring out how to accommodate a vegan, a keto, and a celiac, for example, can feel like a brain twister. It requires time.
- Start preparations the day before *minimum*.
- Do everything possible in advance so you're not dashing around.
- Make sure your house/apartment is clean (at least the living room and bathroom).
- Make a written game plan, starting with what you're going to do during the day or days leading up to your dinner. Be very specific about what steps you will take once guests arrive, e.g., 7:30 p.m.: heat oven to 350 degrees; 7:45 p.m.: ____. It will calm you down to follow instructions that you've already laid out for yourself.
- Set the table in advance. One less thing to stress about.
- Better yet, have the first course plated and ready to be brought to the table, or already on the table when guests arrive (if it is pretty and meant to be served at room temperature).
- For the main course, serve nothing that can't be made ahead except for a few finishing touches. That doesn't mean reheating leftovers, but there are

cookbooks designed to address just this issue (Ina Garten's *Make It Ahead*, for example).

- Make sure all the food comes out at the same time (e.g., side dishes along with the main course).
- Don't plan to serve something you've never cooked before.
- Don't wear all white.
- Don't cook something that could smoke up your apartment.
- Choose music and adjust lighting (including candles) in advance.
- Deputize tasks like pouring wine to select guests—I leave the corkscrew next to the bottle.
- Don't forget to breathe! You've got this!

The cringeworthy scene in which a couple botches an over-ambitious dinner party for the boss and his wife is a TV trope that is only funny on television. To avoid such disastrously stilted evenings, stick with dishes you feel comfortable cooking. I learned this the hard way.

I decided to make risotto for the first time at a dinner party for four very discerning guests I had never met before. My boyfriend persisted in questioning me. "Are you sure? Have you ever made it before?" "No," I said, "but how hard could it be?" (The answer? Impossibly hard. Risotto is one of the trickiest possible dishes to get right.)

The kitchen was open to the living room, which was both a good and a bad thing. On one hand, the "risotto" didn't take me away from my guests for an hour. On the other, they watched me as I stirred, and stirred, and stirred while the "risotto" stubbornly refused to turn into risotto. At last, I gave up. Luckily, there was steak, which my control freak boyfriend cooked every time we had people over and had mastered down to the second.

The only thing over which you have no control is when your guests arrive. There are those who show up late, those who show up early, and even those who show up uninvited (although that's rare for a dinner party). If guests are beyond twenty minutes late and it's a small group dinner, it's permissible to send them a text message asking where they are, or their ETA (if they haven't already messaged you first, which they really should). If they will be arriving beyond half an hour late, start without them. Don't sacrifice the good of the group for a rude latecomer. You don't want hangry guests!

As far as arrival expectations go, it's very important to understand what culture your guests are from. In business school, I had a group of eight closest friends, and each of us was from a different country. The German always showed up right on the dot. The Singaporean, Turk, and I always arrived within ten minutes of the stated time. Our Middle Eastern friends appeared half an hour later. What is considered terribly late in one culture is regarded as on time in another. In her fascinating book *The Culture Map*, Erin Meyer explains that the United States, Germany, Scandinavia, and the United Kingdom have a "linear time" culture. The Middle East, Africa, India, and South America have a "flexible time" culture, in which delays are expected and built into arrival estimates. Other countries fall somewhere in between.

The only thing more inconsiderate than showing up late—globally—is showing up early, because that is when the host is at their busiest—getting dressed, setting the table, making last-minute arrangements. I always open the door a little flustered when people are early, and my response has varied. If I'm not too irritated, I might say, "Oh! Did I send you the wrong time?! Well please come on in, if you don't mind helping me out in the kitchen." If I'm in a disciplining mood, I'll say, "Goodness you're so early! The house isn't quite presentable yet, but there are some delightful boutiques and cafés on my street. Why don't you visit them and come back in an hour?" Some guests, in their desire to be punctual, may arrive a few minutes early. That's why as a host it is better to be ready a little early, as your guests will feel very embarrassed if you aren't ready to receive them. Arriving a few minutes early is forgivable, but significantly earlier is not.

> **Pro Tip:** There are washable wine glass markers you can order so people can write their names on their glass. This works really well if you have six people and up. That way people don't lose track as they move from the living room to the table. It saves a lot of cleanup!

When everyone has arrived and is settled, it's all about the conversation. I always say, "Guests are like a rose. You have to help them blossom." And that means, of course, that a savvy host never dominates the conversation. You are the conductor of an orchestra—prodding the strings and muting the horns in pursuit of a balanced sound. I am not a proponent of avoiding politics or religion at the dinner table. You can't live on a diet of small talk alone. I love talking about politics because that gets people

251

riled up and lends energy to the conversation. People like being pushed beyond their comfort zone. They find it energizing.

However, if you're going to encourage passionate discussion, you'll need to creatively cultivate the art of neutralizing tensions when tempers flare. There is a toxic tendency these days for people to believe that those with whom they disagree are not merely wrong but evil. Ideally, you should intervene before people are ready to come to actual blows. Try asking one of the arguing parties a question designed to slow down the fast-raging exchange of the debate, something that requires facts and isn't open to interpretation. Pretend you need background so that you yourself can understand what's being discussed (or better yet, make the question an authentic one).

I'm assuming that by now experience has taught you that the more emotional you get in an argument, the more you look like a fool and the more the other person looks wise. It's not elegant to get too vehement, mostly because one of the precepts of etiquette is that a person and their feelings are of primary importance and an "opinion" is secondary.

If your clever questions don't do the trick, humor is always a great solution. Since humor is situational, I can't offer any specifics, just make sure not to tease someone who's already feeling thin-skinned! Failing that, simply interrupt, the way you would tap a naughty kitten on the nose, with a line like, "I didn't anticipate the sparks that would fly from this conversation!" Then immediately change the subject to something superficial that everyone will have an opinion about. "Well then, has everybody seen [Netflix series of the month]?" Or suggest playing my favorite game at the dinner table for getting people to open up and engage: Two Truths and a Lie. It helps to spotlight everyone, even those who are a little shy. Whoever guesses wrong drinks! As the host, take your turn last.

Don't Cry over Spilled Milk (or Wine)

If a guest makes a mistake, it's your duty as a host to minimize it—no matter how much it hurts. From the moment a guest crosses your doorstep, their well-being is your responsibility, and that includes their feelings. I remember as a child watching my mother host at home. Once a guest knocked over a full glass of red wine on our living room carpet and immediately turned red with embarrassment, while all the other guests turned to see how my mother would react. "At every dinner party someone has to

> "A host is like a general: it takes a mishap to reveal his genius."
>
> —HORACE

spill wine—now that you've done it, the rest of us can all relax," she chuckled. And she immediately turned to the guest sitting farthest from the spill and asked an open question—"Harry, didn't you just go to Burma recently? It seems like such a mysterious place. Tell us about it." When Harry answered, my mother subtly attended to the spill.

The same goes when someone breaks something. At a small dinner party I threw recently, my friend broke a Bernardaud plate while helping to bring it back into the kitchen. She felt terrible and said, "This must be a really expensive plate." I said, "Don't be silly. It's just a plate. How expensive could it be?" A few minutes later, lingering in the kitchen as I rinsed the dishes, she said, "Oh, it's part of a set!" Again I reassured her, lying through my teeth. "Don't worry! Plates are made to be broken." But inside my heart was bleeding next to my shattered white Bernardaud plate on the kitchen floor.

Since ancient times, the responsibilities of a host have been sacred. People's feelings are more important than physical things. Repeat that like a mantra when your plate hits the floor.

In fact, politeness is a sort of battle. The host's role is to insist on downplaying the damage while the guest's is to insist on making up for it. Even if my friend could not replace my plate, she could have sent something else—even a token gift—as a gesture.

Formal Dinners

Formal dinners, unlike the ones we have been describing, are carefully structured events with a clear raison d'être. Whether their purpose is business or social, they have a predetermined seating plan and a precise start and (usually) end time. Many people think it's awkward to open a formal dinner with a few words, but it's actually more awkward not to. The host should not think of it as a speech, because guests need reassurance that the meal has officially begun. Simply thank everyone for coming, tell them to enjoy themselves, and lift a glass in welcome.

Seating plans

Every culture has its own quirks when it comes to table seating, but there are three common styles with designated rules: English, French, and Chinese.

English style

The host and hostess sit at opposite ends of the (usually rectangular) table. The most important female guest is seated to the right of the host, and the most important male guest is seated to the right of the hostess. The second most important pair (whether they come as a pair or you match them as a pair for seating purposes) will be to the left of the host and hostess. This works best for small dinners of ten and under.

French style

The host and hostess sit opposite each other, but in the middle of the (usually rectangular) table. The most important guests are seated to their right and then their left, mixing the genders just like English style, so that guests are seated male, female, male, female. Wives sit next to their husbands every day, so at dinner they want to be seated next to somebody else's husband! The French style is typically used for larger sized dinners, as well as state dinners, so that the hosts and most important guests can sit close together. The downside of this style is that each guest's ranking for the event is apparent, and those sitting all the way at the ends may feel left out. If you can avoid it, never place a woman at the end.

Chinese style

East Asian dining tables are round to represent harmony. The host sits facing the door, and the most important guest next to him, first to his left, then to his right, then to the left of the person on the left, and then to the right of the person on the right, and so on, fanning farther and farther out. It becomes clear that the half of the table closest to the host consists of the most important guests, and the less important guests sit farther away from the host, but since it is a round table everybody feels equally included. The hostess will sit next to the host, or opposite the host, depending on their preference. Unlike Western-style seating, gender is not a factor. But couples are seated together.

The Next Level

Now that you've mastered the basics, you're ready for the more complicated questions.

Afternoon Tea

Sometimes erroneously referred to as "high tea," afternoon tea should evoke images from Jane Austen novels—or even *Alice in Wonderland*. Finger sandwiches (crusts cut off, please), scones with clotted cream, and small cakes or sweets served on a three-tiered tray with the best linen and silver. And, of course, lovely pots of tea.

Some teacup etiquette

To go back to the old-fashioned cutlery metaphor, your teacup and the saucer beneath it are married. Whenever you put your teacup back down after taking a sip, it belongs back on the saucer. If you decide to take your tea with you to sidle over to a friend, hold it by the saucer (with another hand on the ear of the cup to steady it, if needed). And resist the urge to balance your cup by sticking your pinky out—pinkies in always!

Whether to add milk or sugar first is an age-old debate that has trended both ways at different times in history. It is generally accepted to put sugar in tea before milk so that it can dissolve more easily in the hot liquid.

Tricky foods

I teach a course on tricky foods. When the subject was covered on *Mind Your Manners*, I was overwhelmed with inbound requests on social media. Clearly, everyone has been stumped by a tricky food they've had difficulty eating elegantly.

List of foods you can (and should!) eat with your fingers
Asparagus
Artichokes
Bread
Cheese and cold cuts
Corn on the cob
Hamburgers and hot dogs
Olives
Pizza*
Sushi, for the discerning**
Tacos

*In the so-called Forkgate scandal, the brand-new mayor of New York, Bill de Blasio, committed what *Newsweek* called the "inexcusable gaffe" of eating his pizza with a knife and fork.

**Sushi should be lightly dipped *fish side down* into the soy sauce (otherwise the rice soaks up the soy sauce like a sponge and drowns the delicate flavor of the fish).

A soupçon about soup

Your soup spoon is the large one (the smaller one is the teaspoon). Even though the etiquette experts of yesteryear dictated that one must move the spoon away when you eat soup, no one actually does this. However, it is true that you should sip from the side of your spoon (rather than pointing it straight at your mouth as you would a fork). To get the last few drops of soup, it is acceptable to tip the bowl away from you.

After finishing the soup, leave your spoon on the saucer if there is one. If not, leave it directly in the bowl. The position is the same in both cases: handle pointing toward the bottom right-hand quadrant as if you were going to pick up the spoon again.

It is never permissible in Western dining to drink directly from your soup bowl, but it is acceptable in Asia, so if you're in a Japanese restaurant, go ahead and drink your miso soup from the bowl if you'd like.

How to deal with bones

I read somewhere that it's impossible to eat fish with bones without looking thoughtful, which gives you some idea of the concentration involved. Sometimes a fish is incompletely or unskillfully filleted. Varieties like trout and shad are nearly impossible to fillet completely. In China, we serve fish whole and say that the cleverest children are the ones who can separate fish bones in their mouths and spit them back out at you. As an adult, after using your tongue to separate out the bones, remove them with your index finger and thumb while *covering your mouth with your fingers of the same hand*. Transfer to the edge of your plate without changing your hand position so nobody can see the offending bones.

Biting down on an unexpected bone in another kind of dish, however, is the same as encountering any other inedible part of a meal (like a bit of fat or gristle). It should be dealt with the same way: if it's small, immediately "go to swallow" without tasting. Once again, this is why my mantra is "Take Small Bites." Wash it down with whatever beverage you're drinking. If you simply cannot swallow your bite and no one is watching, you may delicately spit it out onto your fork and return it to your plate. As a last resort, pretend to wipe your mouth with your napkin and wrap it up. Discreetly ask the server for a replacement napkin.

Wine-drinking etiquette

- In a high-end restaurant, don't pour your own wine, even if the bottle is in an ice bucket next to you or on the table.
- Especially if it's an expensive bottle, it's bad manners not to finish your wine. That's why it's better *not* to start drinking than to have one glass and only drink some of it.
- If you don't want to drink, quietly ask the waiter to remove your wine glass. If you don't want a refill or a top-up, put your hand over your glass.
- When pouring wine, don't fill wine glasses too full.
- If you are pouring your own wine, offer it to others before pouring seconds for yourself.
- When drinking from your wine glass while wearing lipstick, drink from the same place on the rim every time. Do not drink *around* the rim of the glass.
- When toasting, clink "bell to bell" rather than at the rim to reduce the chance of breaking fragile glasses.

Wine snobbery for non–wine drinkers

If you order a bottle of wine in a good restaurant, the server or sommelier will pour a little bit into your glass first and wait for you to taste it and give the nod that it is not "corked" (tainted with a virus that smells like a musty basement) or otherwise off. (In a really fine restaurant, the sommelier will taste it for you.) You don't need to swirl and slurp to "aerate" the wine like some wine snobs you might have seen, or smell the cork.

Always hold your wine glass by the stem. Some people erroneously believe that they should hold a red wine glass by the bowl to "warm" the contents, but the polite assumption is that the restaurant (or your host) has brought the wine to the correct temperature before serving it, which even for red wines is slightly below room temperature. (On the other hand, some French people do hold red wine glasses by the bowl, so when in Paris . . .)

How to open champagne properly

If you're opening champagne or other sparkling wine at home, your goal is not to "pop" the cork as if you were at a nightclub. Remove the foil and untwist the little wire cage, keeping pressure on the cork to make sure it doesn't come out prematurely. Then cover the cork with a kitchen towel or cloth napkin, pointing away from your body (and any other bodies), and gently twist the bottle, not the cork. It should come out with a gentle sigh.

Canapés and passed hors d'oeuvres

Cocktail parties can be the best of all worlds. They're dressy but not formal, with drinks but no real food. You can mingle so you're not stuck talking to one or two people. On the other hand, they can create a lot of anxiety, both social and gastronomical—especially over how to juggle those pesky canapés while holding a glass.

Here are some tips for hors d'oeuvres:
- Use your fingers.
- Never put the skewer back onto the serving plate. Find a cocktail napkin or tissue and put it elsewhere.
- If it looks too tricky, don't eat it.
- If it's yummy, do NOT take two at a time or consecutively.
- Time when you eat—ideally asking someone an open question right beforehand so you have time to chew without having to reply with your mouth full.

FOOD: FAQ

What do I do if I drop my fork or knife?

If you drop a piece of cutlery and can pick it up quickly, you should do so. If you would need to crawl under the table, leave it. If you want to pick it up, and the floor is looking a bit dirty, you can throw your napkin over it before handing it to a server.

What should I do if I am served a course I've never eaten before, and therefore don't know how to eat it? Should I ask how?

The short answer is, as in so many other situations, watch your host.

My nose runs when I eat very spicy food. Do I blow my nose at the table or just sniffle?

Turn to the side and use a tissue or paper napkin. It's disruptive to leave the table but it's also rude to sit there sniffling. And absolutely no blowing your nose in a cloth napkin! How are you going to wipe your mouth?

How do you get the last bit of food off your plate and onto your fork?

You can use your knife or a bit of bread. No fingers unless you're absolutely sure no one is looking.

Which hand should the fork be held in if you are not using a knife?

It should be in your dominant hand and held like a spoon, tines up.

Where do you put your knife and fork during dinner when resting and when finished?

To signal that you are resting (meaning, don't take my plate away), make an upside-down "V" with your fork and knife (with the tines and blade touching at the top of your plate). Fork tines are down and knife blade faces in. When you are finished eating, place your fork and knife close together and parallel, with the tines up and the blade facing in (not facing your neighbor—remember that table manners were originally about preventing violence!).

How do I hide the food that I can't finish? Especially for large portions.

Ideally you can hide with the garnish, but otherwise there's nothing you can do. At a casual restaurant you can take it home. Doggie bags are suitable anywhere except fine dining—in the spirit of environmentalism you don't want to waste.

Is it more polite to call servers by their first names, or just call them miss or sir?

If they introduce themselves, using their first names as much as possible works like a charm to get better service. "Sean, could you

bring me some more butter?" "Sean, could I have some hot water?"
Otherwise, miss or sir is the way to go.

What do you do at a restaurant when someone says, "This is so good! You have to taste it."

If you want to try their dish (or you want to appear high EQ and cement your relationship), have them put a little on your bread plate. If they're about to use their dirty utensils, offer your own, saying, "Use my fork. It's clean." If you don't want to taste their dish, say, "I don't think I'll have any room after this, but I'll have to try your dish next time—it looks delicious!" Sharing is absolutely unacceptable in very fine restaurants where each plate is an artistic creation, visually as well as gastronomically.

What if you drop food on the floor?

If it's not noticeable and it's something dry (like a piece of bread), kick it under your chair. If it's something that is wet or will smush, call the server over (discreetly, if possible) and ask them to handle it. In all cases, you don't want anyone to slip and fall.

What do I do when I spill something on myself?

If the stain is small, pour a drop of water from your glass onto your napkin and dab it quickly. If it's a major spill, call the server over and ask, "Do you have anything for this?" They might bring seltzer and a napkin. Do what you can, but get it over with quickly—thirty seconds maximum, which is longer than you think. If necessary, cover the offending area. Tucking your napkin into your neckline can be charming if you do it with a smile. Accept that it happened and move on without giving it energy and attention.

Someone spilled a glass of red wine all over my shoes at dinner the other night. They are completely ruined. The person apologized but didn't seem very sorry. What should they have done?

If you damage someone's stuff, you must offer to pay to have it cleaned or replaced! It's shocking how few people offer this, and it's appalling that more parents have not drilled it into their children.

How to react if the server drops or spills something on you?

First of all, remember that it wasn't intentional. If they have badly stained or perhaps ruined an item of clothing, say with a smile, "I'll send the restaurant the dry cleaning bill," and see what happens. It's worth a try!

When is the right time to ask to pack food leftovers?

If the meal is being served in courses, tell the server discreetly when they clear the course you can't finish that you will be taking it home at the end of the meal. If there's food left over at the end of a meal, ask servers to pack up the various dishes when they are clearing or when you ask for the check, whichever comes first. Encourage other diners to take food home and make sure they don't feel uncomfortable about it. You could say, "I'd take it myself but I'm traveling," or "The steak was delicious. I'm sure your husband would love it." Again, in very fine restaurants, doggie bags are unacceptable.

Sometimes sushi is served in such big rolls that it's impossible to eat in one bite. Can I cut a piece?

You can never cut sushi. You can only bite. Hold a soup spoon underneath to catch any falling parts and steady it between bites.

Do you eat oysters with your hands or using a fork? I have seen both and am never sure which is correct.

Both hand and fork! Pick up the shell and hold it steady with one hand while you use the oyster fork (tines up) with the other hand to eat the meat. If the oyster won't come loose, put your fork between the meat and shell and twist to loosen the muscle.

How many oysters is it considered acceptable to eat in one sitting?

Six is usually considered the upper limit, but I've watched my grandmother eat two dozen at a time.

How do you eat a very leafy salad?

According to the French you should never cut salad. Fold each leaf into a little packet with your knife and fork. The rest of the world, however, thinks it's fine to cut it into bite-size pieces.

How to act when you accidentally eat or drink something too hot?

I half open my mouth and do some deep breaths to cool it—along with a little wave of my hand to signal why I'm crying. That's why I always say you should take small sips or small bites.

How do you eat a burger at a fine-dining restaurant?

Using hands will score you bonus points, otherwise you risk looking like a priss, depending on whom you're with. Eat a burger the same way you eat a club sandwich: by compressing it. Keep the toothpick in to hold everything together.

How do you properly eat pasta dishes?

If you are anywhere but Italy, it's acceptable to twirl long strands against the side of your tablespoon. In Italy, take fewer strands and twirl them as tightly as you can against the side of your pasta plate (if it has a lip) or bowl. NB: In Italy, pasta is served as a starter rather than a main course.

If you are mid-mouthful and someone asks you a question, do you make them wait while you swallow before replying?

Yes, and try to look thoughtful. One more reason you should take small bites!

How do you get someone to stop speaking with their mouth full?

Say, "Goodness, I'm making you eat and talk at the same time. I'll let you eat first." And then you turn to someone else. If it's just the two of you, start delivering a monologue.

What if I catch the host licking the spoon they're cooking with? Say something or not?

It's bad manners to see something you're not supposed to see, and worse manners to point it out.

What do I do while people are singing "Happy Birthday" to me? I feel so awkward.

At the beginning, you just have to grin and bear it. Look at the cake. As the song nears the end, the best thing to do is close your eyes and pretend you're thinking of your wish.

How to say no to seconds without offending the host?

Say, "Thank you, but what I've had was delicious and I'm very full." And remember, an empty plate is an invitation to more food.

If the host puts out embroidered linen hand towels in the restroom, should I use them? If so, what do I do with them afterward?

Only the next level hostess will prepare a tray of individual cloth towels for you and a wicker basket to dispose of them. The embroidered linen hand towel is one level below. If it's there, it's meant to be used. I leave it on the rack and pat my hands dry on it, leaving it more or less intact.

What about guests asking to help in the kitchen?

Guests should stay out of the kitchen unless they're asked or have bestie status.

Do I have to serve a dessert if a guest brings it (and I haven't asked for it beforehand)?

Yes. I believe you can never have too much dessert. It's always better to look more generous and sumptuous and no better opportunity than dessert.

What do I do if I only want half a serving of dessert? Sometimes it looks delicious and I always eat everything that's put in front of me.

If you want half a dessert, tell the host and they'll serve you a smaller portion. Whatever you do, don't share one serving using the same plate and cutlery if you're part of a couple. Using the same dessert plate and fork is on par with excessive PDA.

Do you have to put flowers on the table if a guest brings them?

Put them on the dining table unless they're tall and would obstruct the conversation. In that case put them in the most conspicuous place the guests can see them.

What is the proper way the toilet paper should face in the restroom? Is it over or under?

Over! So many people get it wrong. Because when it's over, it's easier to pull. (A clever reminder is "a beard is always cooler than a mullet.") On the other hand, "over" doesn't work if you have cats! Cats are hunters, so they can't resist something fluttering around in the air, like the edge of the toilet paper roll. Reversing the roll so it dispenses from underneath, while incorrect, minimizes the chances you'll find your bathroom decorated with toilet paper streamers.

What happens when guests move place cards?

This is one of the rudest moves I have seen at a formal dinner. Table seating is painstakingly and intentionally planned by the host. Who are we, as a guest, to disrupt a host's planning? If you are witness to such bad behavior, inform a server to change it back, and if you know the offending party, shame them publicly by joking loudly, "My goodness, did I really see you move your place card? I'm not sure [host's name] will approve of that!"

Should we serve other guests at formal meals?

Not if it is a staffed, sit-down meal—unless you want to offer the bread basket or pour wine before you help yourself. If it is a formal dinner party served family style, you can offer to serve those seated far from a particular dish. Don't overdo it, though, as many like to help themselves. PS: Technically speaking, you're not supposed to eat your bread until the first course appears.

Is it rude to rest your elbows on the dining table, even after a meal?

The no-elbows principle is meant to keep diners from violating the space of those sitting on either side. In primitive societies, not respecting the boundaries of your "place" at the table was seen as a possible threat. Now the rule, even according to strict etiquette experts like Emily Post, is more accurately stated, "No elbows on the table while you're eating." You don't want to intrude on other people's space, but if plates are cleared it's fine.

How do I seat an odd number of people around the table without it feeling awkward?

Seat an even number of people facing each other and put the odd person at the end. According to feng shui principles, you want to enclose the space because it will capture the ren qi ("people energy") and create a more successful dinner.

What do I say if someone asks, "Why are you not drinking?" and I don't want to share the real reason?

In China, the free pass is to say, "I'm taking herbal medicine," since people really respect traditional Chinese medicine. In the US you can say, "I'm on antibiotics." I like to say casually, "I'm not drinking tonight," and then ask the server to remove my glass. If people persist, I've been known to look them in the eye and say, "I'm pregnant."

What wine suits what dish?

Traditionally, red wine with meat and white wine with fish or chicken.

With fish, you can also serve sparkling wine. Generally, wine is not served with soup, so if you have that as a first course, don't pour the wine until the main course. As with most things, only break the rules if you know them.

How do I keep my teeth and lips clean when drinking red wine?
Drink using the inside of your lip. As for your teeth, that's a problem. Drink white wine or rosé instead.

TRAVEL

Being your best self while traveling depends on knowing this golden rule: you are a guest and the locals are your hosts. Focus less on your phone and more on your surroundings. Leave yourself open to chance and serendipity, and that includes food and meetings with helpful strangers (be smart, of course, and don't leave yourself open to being hustled by "friendly" fraudsters). In my opinion, there's nothing better than just wandering in a new city soaking up the atmosphere.

It's important to draw the distinction between travel—which sharpens our senses and awareness—and tourism. If you're really traveling, nothing is automatic, not even ordinary things like getting a cup of coffee or finding a restroom. You can't go on autopilot, which is where you spend most of your time at home. For tourists, on the other hand, everything is preplanned to protect them from effort and anxiety and to ensure that they are never startled by anything new. The result is that tourists replace one set of monotonous routines with another. They return from vacation with the reassuring delusion that how people speak, behave, and eat "at home" is the best way. Don't bring the old you along like a turtle with its shell! It's only when you leave home that you get some perspective on your own culture. Travel is all about clearing away preconceptions, so this final journey of our book takes a different shape from the previous ones. The last thing travelers need is more baggage in the form of precepts and directives. Here's what they do need: an open mind and answers to a seemingly inexhaustible list of questions. So let's get packing.

Air Travel Etiquette

Air travel is not travel; it's torture. No wonder I get more inbound questions on social media about airplane etiquette than almost any other subject. The airplane is the twenty-first-century version of the primordial table: a site of potential violence where people are packed in an enclosed space and explosions can occur from invasions of territory. Here are the most commonly asked travel etiquette questions of all:

Who gets the middle arm rests?

Technically, the person in the middle gets both armrests since the person on the aisle and the person by the window each have one, along with some additional room to move. But it doesn't seem to work that way in real life. Armrests are community property and need to be negotiated, but let me give you a secret tip: once you nudge someone else's elbow, they reflexively move away.

What happens when a rather large person takes over one's real estate when sitting in a seat?

Out of earshot, you can discreetly request a different seat from the flight attendant. If the flight is full, a little kindness goes a long way. Try to have empathy for the larger person, who is probably not doing it on purpose. Smile and request politely, "Could we each please keep our arms inside our own seats?"

Can I take my shoes off on the plane? I am wearing socks!

You should, actually, as your feet are likely to swell. The floor of the plane is really filthy, though. So if an airplane doesn't provide slippers, either bring your own or an extra pair of socks you don't mind getting dirty.

Leggings on board the plane? Comfortable but inappropriate?

I'm all for comfort, but wearing loose clothing is preferred because tight clothes will restrict your circulation, especially when flying long haul.

How to use the restroom on the plane when the passenger next to you is sleeping?

If you have to use the restroom often, make sure to ask for an aisle seat. If you have to climb over someone, try to do it without waking them, but if you must, a gentle tap is best. It's just one of the many indignities of air travel.

If you're sitting in economy class, is it rude to the person behind you to recline your seat?

You can recline a little bit without disturbing anyone, but if you want to recline all the way, do it gradually in case the person behind you has a beverage on their tray table.

How to tell someone behind you to stop kicking or nudging your seat?

You should glance back and make eye contact, which should be enough to make them mindful or even apologetic. If they don't get the hint, ask them once politely. Worst-case scenario, appeal to a higher authority and let the flight attendant tell them off.

On the plane, how should you react to a crying baby sitting next to you? Especially if you feel annoyed?

Do nothing or look empathetic. Think of it as a character-building exercise. Babies cry in planes because their tiny eustachian tubes can't take pressure changes—in other words, they're in pain. And so are their parents. Do you think they are unaware that their screaming infant has made them the target of hatred of everyone on the plane? Do you think that glaring will point something out that they don't already know? If not, use earplugs, noise-canceling headphones, and the mantra, "Thank God I'm not the one with the crying baby." Someday it might be your turn. Karma's a bitch.

How do you decline someone who wants to switch seats with you when they say they want to sit with family? Sometimes they become aggressive.

Say, "I'm sorry, I specifically chose this seat. Maybe you can find someone else?" Redirect. If that doesn't work, call the flight attendant. They're trained for these situations, and you've done nothing wrong. Remember, you want to defuse any possibility of violence.

How should I start a conversation with a stranger sitting next to me?
Commiserate over something. There's always something to complain about on an airplane. Then change the subject to something positive. Make sure the conversation doesn't go on too long, especially if you initiated it.

How do you politely remove yourself from a conversation with a chatty seat neighbor?
That's what eye masks are for! You can always take it off after five minutes or so. (If you don't have an eye mask, earbuds or earplugs will do in a pinch if you make a big show of putting them in.) I like to say, "Well it was good chatting with you. I'm going to settle into a movie/rest for a bit."

Can you wear light fragrance when traveling in close quarters?
Everything is magnified on a plane, so it's best to save it for your arrival. Some people are sensitive.

Is it rude to do your skin-care routine on the plane if you are flying economy and there isn't much room (e.g., a facial mask)?
Yes! It's akin to clipping your nails in public, and economy class is very public. Save your private hygiene for behind closed doors.

Is mile-high ever appropriate under any circumstance?
This is on a lot of people's bucket lists, and one school of thought is that you should try everything once. Two caveats, however.

Don't think you're fooling the flight attendants, or other passengers, for that matter. And, it is a federal offense for which people have been arrested.

> If the airplane is hell, the airline terminal is purgatory. There are few things more maddening than being confined with your carry-on across from someone bellowing or shrieking into their cell phone. Do they have any idea how annoying they are? Do they care? If you must talk on your phone for more than a minute or two, make like a smoker back in the day and find a quiet corner. If you're stuck next to this person, lean over and let them see you staring them down. If they avoid your eye, tap them on the shoulder and put your finger to your lips with a charming smile.

Hotel Etiquette

Hotels present a minefield of small anxieties! Read on so you can rest easy in your home away from home.

How should I leave my hotel room when I check out?

It doesn't have to be tidy, but towels should be on the bathroom floor (I like to put them in the tub) and garbage should be in the garbage can. Return furniture to its original position but don't make the bed. A story we were told at finishing school was that on official visits, the queen of a certain Middle Eastern country would personally inspect the hotel rooms of her entourage before checking out.

Is it okay to take the free toiletries home from hotels?
Why not? You paid for them and they're great for travel.

Do you tip housekeeping staff in a hotel? What is the appropriate amount?
In the US, three to five dollars per night. In Europe, basically the equivalent. Asia is not a tipping culture.

When is the best time to tip people who clean the room? Every day or just at the end of your trip?
Every day, because the staff changes.

Where do I leave the tips for the chambermaid in the hotel in US and Europe?
Clearly visible and tucked under the edge of the pillow. The one exception to tipping the housekeeping staff is England—they don't want you to!

Tipping

There is a spectrum of tipping across cultures: from North America at one end, where you're expected to tip generously for most things, to China and South Korea, which are no-tipping cultures. In Australia, Denmark, Norway, Sweden, Finland, and Iceland, tipping is generally not expected or necessary. Other countries fall somewhere in the middle. Google your destination before you go for detailed information, and when in doubt, tip 10 percent.

Should I tip using cash or write it on the credit card?

Tip in cash and the server will remember you forever. They won't have to wait until the end of the night to get their tip, and they won't have to declare it on their taxes!

General Travel

Here, from a friend who has traveled extensively, is a short list of topics to research before booking a trip. Although it is not exhaustive, it is a useful start:

- Visa requirements
- Safety issues (travel.state.gov is an official US website that lists travel advisories for various countries)
- Climate (including weather for the season you're traveling in). Especially if a trip seems too good to be true, make sure it's not the rainy season, or hurricane season, or unbearably hot or cold during the dates you're considering
- Any local holidays that fall during your trip, when things are likely to be closed
- Festivals, conferences, or special events that might be taking place—both because you might want to participate and because hotels might be booked
- Any shots or vaccinations you might need in advance (sometimes months ahead of time); vaccination requirements for entry/exit
- Available medical facilities, if you have health issues
- Sites of interest, local food, places off the beaten track

Should you try to speak the local language if you are not fluent?

Attempting a local language—even a few words here and there—will always endear you to your listeners. Don't let the fear of making mistakes hinder you, and be grateful when locals help correct you. Learning to speak a culture's language is the first step to better understanding it. At the very least, learn to say hello, please, thank you, and goodbye.

If you are staying with a friend but want to go off on your own, how do you politely leave?

If you've signed up to travel as a pair, then it's hard to ditch your friend—unless you want to do something they aren't interested in. In this case, you can say, "I'm going to take an hour to explore the antique market. I'll come back before dinner."

Dress Code

When traveling, try to respect local dress and customs as far as you can. If you are visiting a conservative country then pack your wardrobe accordingly. Exposing your shoulders or knees in India, for example, will draw unwanted attention from locals. Dressing in local garb, however, is not fitting unless you have a good reason or feel comfortable doing so. Sometimes the best you can hope for is to be invisible and blend in. To be mistaken for a local is always a thrill, even if it's only by another tourist asking for directions!

Is it culturally appropriate to wear ethnic clothes and jewelry, just for a picture?

Cultural dress experiences have become very popular with both foreign and domestic tourists in Asia, for example, but many

Westerners are uncomfortable about the issue of cultural appropriation. As always, context is key. If you are being invited to take part in order to experience another culture more deeply, it would—paradoxically—be presumptuous of you to judge what is appropriate and what is appropriation!

Dining While Traveling

It's important to remember that there are cultural differences in dining etiquette around the globe, as there are in every other area of behavior. A friend recounted that at a casual lunch with their tour guide in Rajasthan, India, she shared a bite of food with her husband by handing him her fork. The guide visibly shuddered (after having licked his own fingers clean very neatly one by one!).

How to manage if you are offered local food but don't like it?

Take a small portion and leave it unfinished on your plate. It is more polite to show that you tried it and didn't like it than to refuse to taste it.

Is it offensive to ask for a knife and fork in a chopsticks eating country?

Looking like you are trying will always win brownie points. Even more if you acknowledge your beginner status and ask the locals for instruction. If you are a lost cause, ask for a spoon and use it together with your chopsticks to push food onto the spoon.

What to do when a culture doesn't cater to vegans?

Being a vegetarian while traveling is relatively easy; being vegan is a challenge. You can get a vegan meal on the plane, but after that it becomes more difficult. Some countries are more hospitable than others. Plan ahead. Bring your own snacks and condiments.

There are websites that list vegan restaurants and grocery stores around the world.

What Is the Fastest Way to Get Immersed in a New Country?

Two things will make you feel part of a new culture quickly: Ask a local to teach you how to pronounce "hello" and "thank you" properly and use them often. And eat the local breakfast rather than whatever you're used to back home. When you start your day this way, your body will know you've truly arrived.

FOOD AND TRAVEL: DIGITAL ETIQUETTE

Food Photography

If you've ever had your hand slapped as you were about to dig into something delicious and heard, "The camera eats first!" you know that we now want proof of a pleasure that used to be considered fleeting.

Just because photographing our food is near-universal behavior doesn't mean it isn't governed by the rules of etiquette. While it used to be frowned upon, the rule in even the most high-toned establishments is now be discreet. Unless there is a "no photo" policy, which will be clearly

"Noncooks think it's silly to invest two hours' work in two minutes' enjoyment; but if cooking is evanescent, so is the ballet."

—JULIA CHILD

displayed on the menu or elsewhere, a photo snapped in under two seconds is permissible so long as you're not using flash or otherwise affecting other tables.

I'm guilty myself of turning meals into photo shoots, but as with everything else, culture and context are key.

Travel Photos on Social Media

In the pre digital age, people subjected others to their travel photos in the form of slideshows or photo albums—assembled *after* they returned from a trip. Now they bombard us in real time. Photos of random stray dogs and monuments with no scale or context. Of their feet. Of sunsets. Of their feet in the sunset. It's as if they—that is, we—have no self-control whatsoever. As many people have said, with great technology comes great responsibility.

What is selfie etiquette at tourist attraction sites?
So long as you aren't ruining anyone else's or smacking of vanity, taking a selfie doesn't hurt anybody. Just remember, no flash photography for museum-grade artifacts or delicate objects.

Is it okay to ask a stranger to take a photo?
Yes, but you are limited to one retake.

I myself enjoy posting my travels, but there's a caveat. According to *Time* magazine, 78 percent of burglars use social media to plan their next break-in. What's worse, insurance companies are increasingly rejecting claims of those whose houses have been burglarized while they were traveling if they posted the fact on social media. You could even be compromising your personal safety while you are away if criminals know where you are staying, especially if you are a woman traveling alone.

Here are a few friendly reminders about what not to do to your helpless followers the next time you're lucky enough to go on vacation:

- Two bent knees with a pool in the background is getting old.
- You get one sunset.
- And one photo of each meal.
- Don't document bad behavior (e.g., posting a picture of yourself climbing all over a heritage monument).
- Limit hashtags, especially #Blessed.
- Taking photos of impoverished people is unethical.
- Taking pictures of deities in religious spaces is disrespectful (e.g., Buddhas in temples, statues in churches).

Try to remember why you went on the trip in the first place!

"We travel, some of us forever, to seek other states, other lives, other souls."

—ANAÏS NIN

EPILOGUE

D eveloping social fluency—and presenting your best self anywhere—is all about feeling at ease in your own skin. Now that you've learned to "mind your manners," you can go forth and navigate any situation with confidence. Contemporary etiquette is about rediscovering the genuine pleasure of a smooth social interaction, comfortably shifting the focus from yourself onto others, and remembering what a sense of community feels like.

The tools and advice, tips, and strategies in these pages will transform your life, and the joy of social fluency will be yours: the deep contentment that comes from winning friends . . . and keeping them.

EPILOGUE

ACKNOWLEDGMENTS

Thank you to Donovan Chan, Jocelyn Little, and Jessica Lee for discovering me and parlaying my career into what it is today. Aside from my mother, no one has pushed me harder to reach my fullest potential than Donovan, who has become not just my producer and collaborator, but a friend, teacher, and mentor. It was Donovan who, as I sat aimlessly in my apartment during a sixty-day COVID lockdown in Shanghai in 2022, recommended I start writing a book.

Thank you to Jill Grinberg, my literary agent, and Denise Page for believing in me and what this book could be. Those magical Shanghai-New York calls as we shaped our ideas were challenging and delightful.

To my publisher, Lauren Marino, and Niyati Patel at Hachette, your patience and insights led us across the finish line. Thank you for placing your confidence in me and giving me an opportunity to share my thoughts on paper with the world.

To my Netflix family, Brandon Riegg, Derek Wan, and Caroline Abaecheta-Smith, thank you for seeing my work in etiquette in all its entirety—as the utmost form of wellness and a way to promote genuine and healthy individual growth. Thank you in particular to Derek for championing *Mind Your Manners* from day one.

Thank you to my agent, Julie Choi, for having more in store for me than I could ever imagine.

To my besties, who are scattered around the world—you know who you are. Thank you for being there for me at different stages of my life.

Thank you to my various mentors at various stages of my career, especially Joe Perella.

Thank you to my family—in particular my closest cousins, Adrianne, Gerran, Fiona, and Sandrine. My mother is gone but she lives and breathes in this book. To my grandmother, who is one of the most amazing women in my life. To my father, principled and kindhearted, who keeps me on the straight and narrow while encouraging me to live life curiously and to the fullest. And to my stepmother for quietly supporting me in all that I do.

To my husband, whose love gives me the strength to achieve anything. Thank you for showing me what it means to love and be loved.

And last but not least, thank you, Dawn Drzal. Months of your late nights and my early mornings spent on the book as we put pen to paper and made it better with each turn were both exhilarating and cathartic for me. We laughed, we cried, we grew together in the process. I couldn't have chosen a better partner than you for this project.